When Children Don't Learn

STUDENT FAILURE AND THE
CULTURE OF TEACHING

EDITED BY BARRY M. FRANKLIN

TEACHERS COLLEGE PRESS

Teachers College, Columbia University
New York and London

Published by Teachers College Press, 1234 Amsterdam Avenue, New York, NY 10027

Excerpts from *The Old Curiosity Shop* by Charles Dickens reprinted by permission of Oxford University Press.

An earlier version of Chapter 3 appeared in Chapters 3–7 of *Caring for Kids: A Critical Study of Urban School Leavers* by Richard J. Altenbaugh, David E. Engel, and Don T. Martin (London: Falmer Press, 1995). Adapted by permission of Falmer Press.

Library of Congress Cataloging-in-Publication Data

When children don't learn : student failure and the culture of
  teaching / edited by Barry M. Franklin.
     p.   cm.
  Includes bibliographical references and index.
  ISBN 0-8077-3719-4 (cloth : alk. paper). — ISBN 0-8077-3718-6
(pbk. : alk. paper)
     1. Academic achievement—United States—Psychological aspects.
  2. School failure—Social aspects—United States. 3. Teacher-
  student relationships—United States. 4. Effective teaching—
  United States. I. Franklin, Barry M.
  LB1062.6.W55   1998
  371.102'0973—dc21   97-51276

ISBN 0-8077-3718-6 (paper)
ISBN 0-8077-3719-4 (cloth)

Printed on acid-free paper
Manufactured in the United States of America

05 04 03 02 01 00 99 98   8 7 6 5 4 3 2 1

Contents

Childhood Failure and the Classroom Teacher

BARRY M. FRANKLIN

Among the problems facing American public education, probably none is more pervasive, persistent, or pressing than teaching children whose attempts at learning result in failure. Sometimes bearing such labels as "slow learner," "low achiever," "underachiever," "retarded," and, most recently, "at risk," but more often overlooked, such children have been a constant presence in American schools. They exhibit their difficulties in a myriad of ways, including substandard performance in reading, mathematics, and other school subjects; inappropriate social behavior; and withdrawal from school. Any reading of today's dropout statistics and proficiency test scores, particularly those of minority group children and children living in poverty, would suggest that academic failure is in fact one of the most intractable problems facing contemporary schools (National Center for Educational Statistics, 1996; Natriello, McDill, & Pallas, 1990).

For teachers, especially, learning failure has a particular importance. At the heart of teaching, Willard Waller noted some 60 years ago, is the fact that teachers must compel their students to learn. "Students," he pointed out, "must learn many things they do not wish to learn, and they must over-learn ad nauseam even the things that originally interested them." "Teachers," he went on to say, "must be task-masters" (Waller, 1965, p. 355). Failure to learn represents a virtual assault on the very act of teaching and on the work of those whose identities are subsumed in that role. The purpose of this volume is to explore the interplay between childhood academic failure and the culture of teaching.

There is, as it turns out, a large body of research dealing with the relationship between teaching and student achievement (Brophy & Good, 1986;

Corno & Snow, 1986; Dusek, 1985). Although much of this work addresses the problem of failure, it often seems to miss what is really important about the experience of student failure for teachers, namely, how such events construct and structure their work lives. Conducted almost exclusively by educational psychologists, this research focuses on the role that teacher behavior, including the instructional strategies that teachers employ, plays as an antecedent to learning success and failure. Such studies typically look at teaching and classrooms from afar through the expert lens of the psychometrician. This is research that rarely gets close to teachers, to children, or to classrooms, that does not include the voices of teachers and children, and that fails to ask how teachers and children understand and make sense of the question of failure. It is, in other words, a body of research that ignores the role that failure plays as one event in the larger culture of teaching.[1]

More helpful in getting closer to the actual classroom experiences of teachers, particularly their encounters with students, is the growing body of ethnographic research on teaching and teachers' lives. Ethnographers are clearly interested in both the work and personal lives of teachers and the problem of academic failure. Yet, they typically consider these two problems separately. There have been few, if any, studies that explore the intersection of childhood academic failure and teachers' work lives. It is this terrain that constitutes the subject of this volume.

Most contemporary research on low achievement assumes a rather traditional notion of school failure as an objective inadequacy. Such a viewpoint equates failure with a gap between student performance and expectations. Or it points to the deficiencies of teaching strategies or curriculum materials. So conceptualized, we have a neat and precise picture of failure. The resulting understanding, however, misses something important. It ignores the experience of failure and how confronting that experience structures and constructs one's life. Failure in this sense is not neat but messy, not precise but inexact. It is, as the essayist and poet Bill Holm suggests, something that intrudes as a myriad of elements that make up our lives:

> In the meantime, I aged from twenty to forty, found myself for all practical purposes a failure, and settled almost contently back into the same rural town which I tried so fiercely to escape. I could not help noticing that personal and professional failure were not my private bailiwick. I know almost no one still on their first marriage, friends, too, were short of money and doing work that at twenty they would have thought demeaning or tedious, children were not such an unpremeditated joy as maiden aunts led us to expect, and for the precocious middle aged, health and physical beauty had begun to fail. It looked as the old cliche had it, as if we were going to die after all, and the procedures would not be quite so character-building as the *Reader's Digest* or the Lutheran ministers implied.

As Holm sees it, failure is a kind of "music" that provides a haunting back-drop to our day-to-day lives:

> Heard from inside, the music of failure sounded not the loudest, gayest marches for cornets and drums, but a melancholy cello, strings slowly loos-ening, melody growing flaccid receding toward silence. The country closed its ears against the tune; citizens denied that they had ever heard it. "Tomor-row," they said, but this was only another way of saying "yesterday," which did not exist quite as they imagined it. This continued denial gave a hollow, whining quality to conversations. Discussion of politics, work, or marriage sounded like a buzz saw speaking English. (Holm, 1985, p. 85)

Pervading the background of teachers' experience, the prospect of student failure routinely rises to the surface. In their study of a progres-sive, English primary school, Rachel Sharp and Anthony Green note that teachers often label children who are difficult to teach or troublesome to manage as potential failures. "Dull stupid children," in their words, "are those whom the teacher finds it difficult to motivate or interest" (Sharp & Green, 1975, p. 157). These are children, Philip Cusick (1983) tells us, who place added demands on the time and effort of teachers:

> An additional consideration about the class with the lower-achieving student was that so many seemed slow and almost painful. Not only did the teacher have to pull everyone along within the framework of decent personal rela-tions, but he had to overlook a lot that is not disorderly or disrespectful, but is distracting—the coming in late, looking around, walking to the front to get a paper or to the back to sharpen a pencil, the surreptitious eating and putting down of heads. Not only does the teacher have to maintain the frame-work of decent personal relations, he or she has to pull the deviating stu-dent into some cohesiveness and at the same time keep articulating the exper-ience. (pp. 65–66)

The prospect of student failure, Mark Faust notes after teaching for 2 years at New York City's Central Park East Secondary School, is a constant pre-occupation of the classroom teacher. Its continuing presence can lead the teacher to feel, in his words, "oppressed" (Faust, 1993, p. 339).

For the authors contributing to this volume, academic failure appears in a variety of forms. It reveals itself most directly and clearly in instances where students are unable to master the academic content of the curricu-lum or pass required competency tests. It also manifests itself when stu-dents withdraw from school prior to graduation, are labeled at risk or dis-abled, or are placed in special or remedial education programs. Finally, it can be seen when students' race or class backgrounds block their educational progress. Notwithstanding the different ways in which the contributors to this volume define failure, their chapters explore how the prospect of childhood academic failure structures and constructs the work of teaching. Using various forms of qualitative inquiry, these researchers seek to make academic failure problematic and thus subject to analysis and critique.

Lynda Stone (Chapter 1) offers a postmodern philosophical exploration of the language of failure. Stone's starting point is the concept of the "dunce" as used by Charles Dickens in his early 1840s serial, *The Old Curiosity Shop*. Looking at Dickens's depiction of an inept teacher and his unmanageable classroom, Stone introduces her readers to how language, in this case the term *dunce*, can be used to describe failure. Stone uses the insights of a number of postmodern scholars, particularly Michel Foucault, to explore how language serves as a socially constructed vehicle for defining and describing the reality in which we live. She then turns to the language of failure itself, again using the insights of postmodern scholars, to show how teachers have used their discourse to create a virtual field of failure, which she refers to as "Failurism." As Stone sees it, it is this language of failure that teachers use, often unintentionally, to constrict the life destinies of low-achieving children. Likewise, it is the understanding about language and its power that a postmodern philosophical lens offers teachers, that will allow them to overcome the strictures imposed by the language of failure.

In Chapter 2, Barry Franklin explores the concept of teacher heroism through a genealogical examination of the provisions that have been made in twentieth-century American classrooms in response to a variety of forms of student failure. Our contemporary discourse about teaching and teacher education, according to Franklin, seems to attribute much of the willingness and ability of classroom teachers to provide for low achievers to their supposed heroism. That is, they seem willing, often at risk to their careers, to challenge bureaucratic rules, overstep community norms, and embrace pedagogical innovations. Franklin's genealogy identifies five kinds of provisions that twentieth-century American public schools have made for low-achieving children. They include special classes, the introduction of curriculum or organizational modifications into regular classes, the establishment of remedial programs outside of special education, the use of various informal efforts by classroom teachers to help low-achieving children, and the creation of compensatory educational programs to aid culturally disadvantaged, minority youth. Franklin then goes on to explore a number of encounters between classroom teachers and low-achieving children involving each of these five approaches to see what they tell us about the notion of teacher heroism. These encounters, he argues, point to the array of attributes that enter into making a heroic teacher. They include such things as teacher beliefs, skills at curriculum modification, prior training and knowledge, insightful teaching, and just plain luck. Franklin's chapter offers a picture of the diverse ways in which classroom teachers from the turn of the twentieth century through the 1960s sought to accommodate low-achieving children.

In Chapter 3, Richard Altenbaugh looks at student withdrawal from school as a type of academic failure. Using in-depth interviews of 100 students at the Pittsburgh Job Corps Center, he reconstructs the classroom experiences of a group of that city's "school leavers." Predominately African American and from families in poverty, his group of interviewees were quite typical of low-achieving students nationwide. For these informants, Altenbaugh argues, two key attributes displayed by their high school teachers played a major role in their decision to drop out. One such factor was attitudinal and had to do with the care and concern exhibited by teachers. What drove many of these individuals from school was their encounters with teachers who appeared to have little compassion for their students or who showed little interest in their personal lives and academic success. For some of these students, such lack of concern was interpreted as racism on the part of their teachers. The second factor was pedagogical skill. What often led these students to leave school, according to Altenbaugh, was their encounters with teachers who were unable or unwilling to design engaging and challenging learning experiences. Altenbaugh goes on to explore the role that gender plays in the cultivation of such skill. Altenbaugh concludes his chapter by arguing that policy makers must realize the important role that teachers can play in promoting student success and mitigating against academic failure.

Eleanor Blair Hilty (Chapter 4) explores the differing understandings of student failure held by classroom teachers. Using in-depth life and career interviews, Hilty examines how five experienced teachers, three Whites and two Blacks, who have been successful in working with at-risk children, perceive the problem of student failure. As her informants see it, teaching at-risk children is a challenging, often disappointing job. Yet, these teachers seemed to welcome at-risk children into their classrooms and were willing to take responsibility for them. Hilty points out that these teachers were unwilling to accept the inevitability or finality of failure, and consequently they sought to find ways to create environments where at-risk children could learn. One of their key goals, she goes on to say, was to try to overcome the "walls" that they saw as blocking the success of at-risk children. When her informants talked about their students, Hilty notes, they often invoked the term "love" to describe their concern and commitment. For these teachers, working with at-risk children was the source of the challenges that made their work joyful and important.

Hilty points out that the two Black teachers she interviewed seemed particularly frustrated about the high level of academic failure among African American children. Yet they wanted to teach Black students. Black at-risk students were, these teachers argued, part of their community, their culture, and their responsibility. Hilty concludes her chapter by considering what the perceptions of these five teachers tell us about the role that teachers can and should play in addressing the problem of student failure.

In Chapter 5, Susan Peters, Alan Klein, and Catherine Shadwick consider one of the most potent forms of failure in contemporary American schools, placement in special education. Their chapter examines the perceptions about schooling and teachers held by a group of about 40 African American students enrolled in a learning disabilities program in an urban high school. Employing data from formal classroom discussions, informal conversations, and student writing of various types, these authors use the actual voices of learning disabled students to explain what it means to be placed in special education. Our conventional understanding of special education, according to Peters, Klein, and Shadwick, emphasizes the disability of students placed in these programs and their need for help. Their data suggest, however, that students placed in special education are actually quite resilient and resourceful in manipulating an educational system that rarely meets their needs. Embracing the perspective of critical pedagogy, Peters and her colleagues reject the conventional view of a learning disability as a defect within the individual and see it instead as a social construction of the existing school culture and its pattern of expectations and opportunities.

Peters, Klein, and Shadwick introduce three metaphors for interpreting the voices of these students and their struggles for self-respect. Some students, whom they refer to as "street-wise philosophers," recognize the injustices that surround being placed in special education, but understand how such a placement can provide them with the additional help that they need to reach their goals. A second group of students, "image-makers," devote their attention to hiding the fact that they are in special education. And finally there are the "jazz improvisationists," who attempt to take advantage of whatever help they can find in special education to enhance their educational and social success. Peters, Klein, and Shadwick conclude their chapter by exploring what these metaphors tell us about school failure and the appropriate responses on the part of schools and teachers.

Susan Merrifield (Chapter 6) examines the failure that accompanies competency testing. As an instructor of freshman English in the early 1980s at what she calls Urban University (UU), an open admissions college in a major northeastern city, Merrifield was responsible for preparing her largely nontraditional, working-class students for a written proficiency examination that all undergraduates had to successfully complete before entering their junior year. The test required students to use a set of readings along with their own background knowledge to write a "relatively polished" essay of about seven to ten paragraphs. It was an examination, Merrifield argues, that demanded not only a high level of writing proficiency on the part of her students but an equally high level of reading ability. Merrifield goes on to detail the steps she took to integrate both reading and writing into her courses to prepare her students for this examination. Relying on her own experiences 2 decades earlier as a student at UU and the insights she obtained as a teacher of whole language in public schools, Merrifield organized her course along themes that she believed were both comprehensible and relevant to the lives of her students. She offers an extended description of one such unit, which she entitled "Growing up Below the Median Income."

Merrifield's thematic approach to instruction resulted in the majority of her students passing the writing examination. But there were students who, despite her efforts, failed. She concludes her chapter by considering what the impact of these failures taught her about herself and her work as a teacher.

Brian DeLany (Chapter 7) shifts our attention from the classroom to the school itself as he examines the failure that results from problems of school organization. Using Stephen Ball's notion of the "micro-politics" of schools as his conceptual framework, DeLany examines data from a case study of resource allocation in four high schools in the San Francisco Bay area. In the study, he examines the processes surrounding the assignment of students to teachers and courses, and considers how the resulting matches affect student and teacher success and failure. Because these assignments often are affected by an array of factors over which schools have little control, including student enrollment, teacher shortages, and state curriculum mandates, the resulting matches are often arbitrary. They regularly lead to disruptions and dislocations in the ongoing operation of schools, which DeLany labels as "turbulence." He argues that schools use the categories of success and failure in an attempt to manage this turbulence.

In Chapter 8, Henry Levin offers some reflections on how educational policy can address the problems of student and teacher failure delineated in this volume. Failure, as Levin sees it, refers to the inability of students to meet certain standards of knowledge and skill set for them by the larger society. Attaining such standards, according to Levin, often emphasizes rote learning and conformity at the expense of creativity and critical thought. Teachers and educational policy makers who confront this issue, Levin argues, have two choices. They can adhere to the currently popular movement toward creating national standards and try to help students meet such expectations. Or they can embrace any of a number of ongoing initiatives for school restructuring that each in their own way seek to fundamentally alter the standards by which we judge student success. Levin favors the latter alternative and in the remainder of his chapter looks at his own Accelerated Schools Movement as an example of how school restructuring addresses problems of student and teacher failure.

NOTE

1. For a review of the research on the culture of teaching, see Feiman-Nemser and Floden (1986).

REFERENCES

Brophy, J. E., & Good, T. L. (1986). Teacher behavior and student achievement. In M. C. Wittrock (Ed.), *Handbook of research on teaching* (3rd ed.; pp. 328–375). New York: Macmillan.

Corno, L., & Snow, R. E. (1986). Adapting teaching to individual differences among learners. In M. C. Wittrock (Ed.), *Handbook of research on teaching* (3rd ed.; pp. 605–629). New York: Macmillan.

Cusick, P. A. (1983). *The egalitarian ideal and the American high school: Studies of three schools.* New York: Longman.

Dusek, J. (Ed.). (1985). *Teacher expectancies.* Hillsdale, NJ: Lawrence Erlbaum.

Faust, M. A. (1993). "It's not a perfect world": Defining success and failure at Central Park East Secondary School. In R. Donmoyer & R. Kos (Eds.), *At-risk students: Portraits, policies, programs, and practices* (pp. 323–341). Albany: State University of New York Press.

Feiman-Nemser, S., & Floden, R. E. (1986). The culture of teaching. In M. S. Wittrock (Ed.), *Handbook of research on teaching* (3rd ed.; pp. 505–526). New York: Macmillan.

Holm, B. (1985). *The music of failure.* Minneapolis: Prairie Grass Press.

National Center for Educational Statistics. (1996). *Digest of educational statistics 1996.* Washington, DC: GPO.

Natriello, G., McDill, E. L., & Pallas, A. M. (1990). *Schooling disadvantaged children: Racing against catastrophe.* New York: Teachers College Press.

Sharp, R., & Green, A. (1975). *Education and social control: A study in progressive primary education.* London: Routledge & Kegan Paul.

Waller, W. (1965). *The sociology of teaching.* New York: Wiley.

CHAPTER 1

Language of Failure

LYNDA STONE

In Dickens's *The Old Curiosity Shop*, a dunce, ironically, is empowered momentarily (as are his peers) by the incapacity of the teacher.[1] The story is of the dark, vagrant travels of Little Nell and her grandfather. Herein are characters of good and evil; here also is the goodness and the evil of English society. At one point as they seek shelter for the night, the wanderers meet a schoolmaster lamenting the illness of his favorite scholar (who subsequently dies). After a safe night, Nell visits the schoolmaster's classroom. Following is a description of what she sees:

> A small white-headed boy with a sunburnt face appeared at the door . . . came in and took his seat upon one of the forms . . . . Soon afterwards another white-headed little boy came straggling in, and after him a red-headed lad . . . and so on until the forms were occupied by a dozen bodys or thereabouts, with heads of every colour but grey and ranging in their ages from four years old to fourteen years or more. . . .
>
> At the top of the first form—the post of honour in the school was the vacant place of the little sick scholar. . . . No boy attempted to violate the sanctity of seat . . . but many a one peered from the idle . . . space to the schoolmaster, and whispered [to] his idle neighbor behind his hand. . . .
>
> Then began the hum of conning over lessons . . . [and] the whispered jest and stealthy game . . . and in the midst of the din sat the poor schoolmaster. . . . The idlest boys . . . growing bolder with impunity, waxed louder and more daring. . . . The puzzled dunce, who stood beside . . . [the schoolmaster's desk] to say his lesson out of book, looked no longer at the ceiling for forgotten words, but drew closer to the master's elbow and boldly cast his eye upon the page. (Dickens, 1841/1951, pp. 187–188; reprinted by permission of Oxford University Press).

The schoolmaster, unable to concentrate on the class events for worry, dismisses the boys and subsequently faces the wrath of the community for his action.

Accompanying the tale is an illustration in which sitting atop a cupboard is a peaked dunce cap, with the understanding that in normal circumstances it is worn by the student who attempts but cannot succeed in his lessons. A failure. This symbolization of the dunce as a school failure is common in America as in England: Depictions almost to this day (in school history books, in remembrances of TV's *Little House on the Prairie*, or others of the same genre) often show a child sitting on a stool in the corner wearing the cap—as a target for ridicule by fellow students.

The scene points to the humanness of classroom life, its vagaries and vicissitudes. It indicates too the central idea of this chapter, that life and language are one; and, in this case, part of a literary discourse—of schooling—and of failure in nineteenth-century English life. The scene also resonates as events of common experience: We know what it means to be a dunce; we hope that we are not this student. To be a dunce means to be a failure, and no one wants this. Across time, the figure of the dunce remains. From where does it come? What does it say about failure?

Dickens's story comes from a literary discourse; experience is put into words and these words function in the specific ways of the novel. The novel is one of many worlds of language. In what follows, some of these worlds are explored. The general thesis is that one aspect of doing something about school failure is to attend to its language, which is a central aspect of intervention.

Before turning to language worlds, something by way of introduction needs to be said about how language functions in education (and in all institutions). First, language use is largely taken for granted. All of us use words, engage in conversation and other language encounters, convey meaning, and attempt at least to fulfill purposes, without questioning the language that we use. Indeed if there is questioning—for instance, a conversational fumbling across mutual intents—language serves as the medium of trial and error. But it is taken for granted and encoded in language practices, which have been described in various ways. Contemporary psychologists such as Robert Sternberg theorize that situations have scripts that are learned and repeatedly enacted; philosophers such as John Searle or Jurgen Habermas develop public speech act theories. Earlier in the century, Ludwig Wittgenstein, also a philosopher, proposed that life itself was a series of language games.[2]

Further, philosopher Charles Taylor claims that this century has been characterized by language preoccupation not only because humans have come to recognize themselves as "language animals," but also because their self-attention (a key feature of the modern world) has pointed out something about themselves and their language. Just as persons are complex and enigmatic, so, too, is language (Taylor, 1985)[3] Building from Wittgenstein and agreeing with Taylor, Richard Rorty calls this enigma the "contingency of language" that accompanies the "contingency of selfhood." From a radical position toward these contingencies, Rorty (1989) writes:

> [We] have no prelinguistic consciousness to which language needs to be adequate, no deep sense of how things are [including ourselves. To be thoroughly Wittgensteinian, we have] simply a disposition to use the language of our ancestors, to worship the corpses of their metaphors. . . . [Today we need] to get to the point . . . where we treat everything—our language . . . [and ourselves] as a product of time and chance. (pp. 21–22)

WORLDS OF LANGUAGE

Talk

Language comes in many forms, forms with different functions. Consider first the talk of teachers. What does it comprise? What are its sources? How does it obtain authority? Teachers talk to their students, to each other, to parents.[4] Some terms are used in all interchanges; others are specific to each one. Teacher talk takes diverse forms from many sources: the ethical words of relationships, the professional jargon of curriculum and learning theory, the communicative competence of public exchange. Such words as *caring*, *development*, and *involvement* have contextualized meanings. When these words are used in contexts other than schooling, say, home or work, they mean something different (at least slightly so).

Discourse

Daily, informal talk is something all recognize. Discourse is a related, less familiar language type. It is the systemic organization of more abstracted language (such as the novel), tied to but often criss-crossing formalized, scholarly, and authoritative disciplines.[5] In the writings of the late French philosopher Michel Foucault, this basic idea of discourse is extended and made more subtle as discursive practices. A primary principle is that all forms of language are "regularities" within systems of thought that designate "exclusions and choices":

> Discursive practices are characterized by a delimitation of a field of objects, the definition of a legitimate perspective for the agent of knowledge, and the

fixing of norms for the elaboration of concepts and theories. . . . [They] are not purely and simply ways of producing discourse. They are . . . [rather] embodied in technical processes, in institutions, in patterns of general behavior, in forms of transmission and diffusion, and in pedagogical forms which, at once, impose and maintain them. (Foucault, 1970/1977a, pp. 199–200)

Language thus is always integral to institutions and their practices, and as a result individualized control is always and strongly constrained. What commonly is assumed in the world in which we live is power over what we say and do; this relationship between agency and language is part of what Foucault problematizes.[6] In the problematization, language is always more, and always bounds: Difference, instead of the more common Anglophone logic of sameness and correspondence, is the organizing function of language. Practices too are defined by what they are not; a practice does not exist, that is, have meaning, unless it is understood in terms of its other.

Vocabulary

Claiming some affinities with Foucault, Rorty adds the idea of vocabularies to the present picture of language. Also tied to practices, these are large ways of making sense of the world. Included within vocabularies are the more systemic and confining discursive practices. Not as large as world views, vocabularies exist within them.[7] At any given time, there are multiple and competing vocabularies, alternative ways some of which will come to dominate, some of which give way to new ways of saying. Evolution and creation are examples, as are Hegel's history and Freud's psychology.

Two aspects of vocabularies are significant. The first is that vocabularies are "tools" for communication, used through what Donald Davidson refers to as "passing theory." Building from Davidson, Rorty explains that communication (incorporating all language functions) occurs as if strangers meet and posit theories about what each other says and does. We "speak the same language" only through "passing"

[as we constantly correct, that is,] allow for mumbles, stumbles, malapropisms, metaphors, tics, seizures, psychotic symptoms, egregious stupidity, strokes of genius, and the like. . . . Davidson's point is that all "two people need, if they are to understand each other . . . [to work across vocabularies] is the ability to converge on passing theories from utterance to utterance." (Rorty, 1989, p. 14)

A second significance is that there are not only general vocabularies but also special, individual contributions that help change vocabularies—

here Rorty posits a stronger notion of agency than does Foucault. Change occurs in two ways: New practices lead to new ways of talking about them, and new ways of talking change practices.[8] Rorty's theory is that most persons are traditionalists, following the vocabularies of their time and place, but some are iconoclasts who introduce "redescriptions." These new ways of conceptualizing arise in irony rather than common sense. For ironists in general, there is doubt about current descriptions of the world (within their own vocabulary) because other vocabularies seem to have something to offer. Rorty (1989) explains:

> [Unique ironic iconoclasts] specialize in redescribing ranges of objects or events in partially neologistic jargon, in the hope of inciting people to adopt and extend that jargon. . . . [The hope is that in] using old words in new senses, not to mention introducing brand-new words, people will no longer ask questions in the old words. (p. 78)

LANGUAGE AND TRUTH

To this point, what Taylor refers to as the enigma of language and some of its forms have been put forth. That language use is complex is obvious once one looks realistically at the conversational ways of life. But this presents a serious dilemma. Many persons want to know what is real, what is certain, what is true. They need anchors upon which to base their everyday decisions and actions. More generally, this search for certainty has been typical not only for modern persons but also for most others across the millennia.

Today, in what is more and more commonly called the "postmodern age," people continue to struggle with both perceived complexity and uncertainty. Many are not comfortable, even longing nostalgically for a more stable past. Others are learning to live better with discomfort, with change and insecurity that some theorists assert have always been "basic" to the human condition. One way to adapt comes from two contemporary theories of truth, pragmatism and poststructuralism. As often put, truth both is underdetermined—it cannot be pinned down—and undermined.

Historical Overview

Across time, truth has and continues to matter in ordinary life as a central touchstone for belief and action. Also in the history of Western thought, language has "mattered" to truth and to philosophy, according to Ian Hacking (1975). Traditionally, language has been the medium by which truth is asserted: "I know that this is a (true) circle," one of the ancients said; "I know that this is the one [true] God," uttered a scholastic centuries later. Across time, then, truth moved from an ideal form to the ideal of God—a change in conception to be sure. More recently, it has been appropriate to speak of truth in the relationship of person to object/world/self and other persons. Various descriptions have been developed, among them: "I know that the idea (internal) in my mind is representative of the (external) object in the world," and even more technically, "I think, therefore I am." In this century, for philosophers (and other scholars too), representational truth has been deemed inappropriate since truth statements cannot actually connect to the world.[9]

Pragmatist Truth

In the first half of the twentieth century, a group of American philosophers, who most notably included William James and John Dewey, proposed a pragmatist theory of truth.[10] Language was still the medium in the interaction of people and their environments, and what Dewey called "warranted assertability" became a synonym for truth. In the earliest formulations, truth was posited after a testing out of principle or act through its consequences and through common agreement about the results of testing. This was an age of experimental instrumentalism (with a strong everyday belief in the value of science) in which a faith existed that "experience will out." Notably, many different kinds of changing warrants were possible, not just the rationalist mathematical logic or the empiricist perception of former times. Pragmatist truth opens up the possibilities of truth claims; paraphrasing Rorty (1989), when "idealistic/realistic" (p. 19) views of truth are altered and language no longer points to either a hidden reality outside or inside persons. When language no longer points, the principal point is that language just is and truth becomes a function of language. Hacking (1975) states that by the late 20th century, a (neo)pragmatist truth means that language is itself that "which constitutes human knowledge" (p. 187).

Even as ordinary persons "talk truth" according to some commonsense standards like experience, authority, and conviction, philosophers have attempted to determine truth's own basis and, connected to it, the base of knowledge as "justified true belief." A long-range view of their efforts indicates that they have been "unsuccessful." Logical responses are three: one, to keep questing for truth's "answer"; two, to posit a kind of realizable ideal, as in the synonym of verisimilitude; or three, to relinquish the search and offer a different kind of explanation for the historical presence of truth. Pragmatist truth is a first step in the last direction, as are the contributions of the early linguistic and anthropological structuralisms.

Poststructuralist Truth

While early American pragmatism begins epistemologically with personal and public experience, continental European theory in approximately the same period begins with language itself and its place in human culture. The move from French structuralist truth to poststructuralist truth has been part of a deprivileging of language—again of recognizing its enigmatic character. Instead of pragmatist truth as a function of the properties of sentences and their relationships to each other, poststructuralist truth (if talked about at all) is even more sociological and linguistic. Foucault's tact is to abstract "truth" as a kind of discursive practice. His point is that "truth is a thing of this world: it is produced only by virtue of multiple forms of constraint. And it induces regular effects of power" (Foucault, 1977/1980b, p. 131). In contemporary societies, it has these traits:

> [It] is centered on the form of scientific discourse and the institutions which produce it; it is subject to constant economic and political incitement (the demand for truth . . .); it is the object . . . of immense diffusion and consumption (circulating through apparatuses of education and information); it is produced and transmitted under the control, dominant if not exclusive, of a few great political and economic apparatuses (university, army, writing, media); lastly, it is the issue of a whole political debate and social confrontation. (Foucault, 1977/1980b, pp. 131–132)

Foucault continues that each society has its "regime of truth," that is, "the types of discourse which it accepts and make[s] function as true." There are also mechanisms by which truth is sanctioned and valued, and that give status to those who speak truth.[11] Finally, the result of Foucault's conception is to alter the traditional notion of truth: No longer is it a property of either the real or the ideal world but is instead a function of language usage given that this usage is relationally effected by discursive and nondiscursive effects and also produces them. These are carried by language but are not directly intended or even recognized.

LANGUAGE OF FAILURE

The upshot of these two postmodern theories of truth is that truth is not absolute or inherent in either its realistic or its idealistic sense. It has become a function of deprivileged language and as such is antifoundational, antiessentialist, and antirepresentational. Further, Foucault's insight is a questioning of the "agency model" of Davidson and Rorty, that is, that people actively construct language.[12] But, do they? Sometimes discursive practices of language take on a life of their own. This life is part and parcel of the history, structure, and function of language itself. Postmodern theories of truth hold that there is no truth to failure. However, this does not mean that failure does not take place and have actual consequences, such as the feelings of well-intended teachers, test scores listed in newspapers, or family strife over such factors as student effort. What a language of failure means is that any search for it is not only futile but meaningless. In Wittgensteinian terms, the language game of truth is a language game.[13]

In this matter of the language of failure, something more can be said about the concept of the dunce and its related practices.[14] First, the meaning of the word has changed over time. "Dunce" has a history related to the thirteenth-century English scholastic theologian-philosopher John Duns Scotus whose writings were dominant for several centuries. After some time, his followers were attacked for their useless, hair-splitting philosophical distinctions. Then, during the sixteenth century, this ridicule was transformed into the sense in which Dickens used the word: a "dull, obstinate person impervious to new learning, a blockhead incapable of learning or scholarship." That this has always been a public attribution of rebuke is significant and continues in the practice of the dunce cap. In more recent connotative evolution, school failures are also classroom troublemakers.[15] Overall, the conclusion to draw from this story is that failure was not always failure; at one time a "duns" was actually a kind of philosopher engaged in a theoretical dispute.

As indicated above, central to the concept of the school dunce is rebuke. The discursive practice of laughter, with its similar history, is related. First, one wonders about the shape of the dunce cap and its own derivation. Is it related to the costume of jesters? One study traces laughter to Renaissance carnival and theater. Hobbes commented: "[Much] laughter . . . [is] at the defects of others, is a sign of Pusillanimity. . . . For of great mind, one of the proper workes is, to help and free others from scorn, and compare themselves only to the most able" (Bristol, 1985, p. 128). Erasmus stated: "[There] was never any pleasant which folly gave not relish to. Inasmuch that if they find no occasion of laughter, they send for 'one that may make it,' or hire some buffoon flatterer, whose discourse may put by the gravity of the company" (p. 131). During this age, laughter was connected with irresoluteness, with cowardice. Further, as the contemporary author Bristol accounts, there are connotations from "seeing someone fall" that are "as universally laughable as the revelation of the lower body" (p. 135), and above all with "consciousness of inferiority and superiority in the individual subject" (p. 128). Philosopher Mikhail Bakhtin explains:

Renaissance theories of laughter all posit a human collective as the precondition of laughter. The social environment in which laughter takes place is complex and highly differentiated. . . . Laughter interprets the complexity of social relations by drawing attention to a structure of difference, especially those "vertically" distributed differences so important to a hierarchy of social positions. . . . [Moreover, the] spontaneous, elusive and "harmless" character of laughter makes it an extremely valuable resource and instrument of any social group that lacks power but seeks to retain a strong feeling of solidarity. (Bristol, 1985, pp. 137–138)

As this example of an archaeology of laughter demonstrates, language in terms of talk, discursive practices, and vocabularies begins with and takes the form of speech or writing. Revealed through Foucauldian historical-philosophical studies, the conception of language operation, influence, and effect is extended. Truth is produced but, as seen subsequently, it is often in terms of subtle and indirect power. There is a pervasive, ubiquitous presence of language in human life. This presence is manifest in the three types of studies conducted by Foucault:[16] Archaeology analyzes relations among discursive forms that are indicative of stratified regulations of knowledge. Basic units are statements exemplified as archives. Building on archaeology, genealogy analyzes nondiscursive forces ("environments") for statements that are illustrative of strategic relations of power. The basic units are scenes abstracted in diagrams, maps of social fields. Internalizing the "exterior" relations of archaeology and genealogy, ethics analyzes relations of self to self, the forming process by which power/knowledge and morality are "innerconnected." Subjectivities as artifacts are basic units manifest as memories.[17]

FIELD OF FAILURE

One need not understand thoroughly or practice Foucauldian histories in order to grasp his point about language. Two ideas seem basic: the first about history itself and the second about relations. For Foucault, history means difference and discontinuity, not sameness and continuity, as the tradition posits. He writes:

In the history of ideas, of thought and of the sciences . . . [mutation] has broken up the long series formed by the progress of consciousness, or the teleology of reason, or the evolution of human thought; it has questioned the themes of convergence and culmination. . . . It has led to the individualization of different series, which are juxtaposed to one another . . . [and which] overlap and intersect . . . [without being reduced] to a linear schema. (Foucault, 1969/1972, p. 8)

Foucault's project has been to rewrite history, to seek out the untold stories for telling. In doing so, his overall method has two aspects, the first of which is the basis of relation. If linearity is given up as an organizing principle, then something takes its place. For Foucault this is relation: History, language, and thus life exist as series/strata/ever-changing forces of relations. The second aspect is a different approach to space and time: Cutting across relations are transversals, as transgressive challenges to the limits of systematized discursive practices.[18] Subversion is dispersion.

One way to understand historical discursive practices is to suggest the creation of a field of failure, failure studies—"failurism" it might be called. The lead for this suggestion comes from the work of culture critic Edward Said, who was influenced by Foucault. Said's passion is "Orientalism," a geographically based systematic study of "the Orient." In the positivity of its creation, ironically, it has been used to subordinate and make inferior the East to the West. Said pointed out:

> Fields, of course, are made. They acquire coherence and integrity in time because scholars devote themselves in different ways to what seems to be a commonly agreed-upon subject matter. Yet it goes without saying that a field of study is rarely as simply defined as even its most committed partisans— usually scholars, professors, experts, and the like—claim it is. Besides a field can change so entirely, in even the most traditional disciplines . . . as to make an all-purpose definition of subject matter almost impossible. (Said, 1978, p. 50)[19]

A return to Foucault helps explain how "discursive fields" develop. Recall from above the constitution of discursive practices through regulatory choices and exclusions. If it can be said that there is a process, it is that ordinary talk becomes repetitive as statements; these utterances and inscriptions become related to others and sedimented as still more complex relations of language. Recall also that language is tied to practices, actions, and institutions. Consider the first use of dunce, the naming in a negative way of a philosopher with a different view. The philosophic context subsequently changed but the negative, exclusionary term remains and is repeated—perhaps in a North American classroom. Dunce statements, moreover, become tied to other statements: for instance, "She is stupid." In the twentieth century, stupidity is related to the construction of intelligence. Mention of intelligence relates the field of failure to psychology: Fields are related to, both incorporate and transverse, more traditionally defined disciplines. Important in the transversals, fields such as Orientalism or failurism recognize marginal "Others." They are, in Foucault's (1976/1980c) term, part of a large "knowledge of anomaly." Recognition of anomaly does something else, of course; it undermines the traditional disciplines by pointing to historical but buried contents and offers opportunity for what Foucault calls an "insurrection of subjugated knowledges." Not only are contents buried but they are disguised. They are "anti-sciences": "local, discontinuous, disqualified, illegitimate knowledges . . . [that allow the rediscovery of the ruptural effects of conflict and struggle] against the claims of a unitary body of theory which would filter, hierarchise and order them in the name of some true knowledge" (p. 83). Importantly, "local" may describe the particular, as in an archival or documentary anecdote, but more pertinently it refers to "the harshness with which it is opposed by everything surrounding it" (p. 82). To Foucault's list of the criminal, the insane, the delinquent, and the sexually deviant, is added the failure.

LANGUAGE/POWER AND FAILURE/SHAME

In Foucault's idiom, the creation of "failurism" is revealed first through archaeological studies as statements/practices such as those of the dunce and its ironic history. There are also possible genealogical and ethical studies. The first are manifest techniques of external power that permeate failure practices; the second internalize power effects as self-regulation. Several distinctions between fields like Orientalism and "failurism" are important. The former has not only regional specificity but also a perspectival orientation. Other places are homes of Others unlike Us. Moreover, there is no danger that we are them. A significant difference, then, is that there is a diffuse locale for failure; significantly, there is personal danger. Because all of us might fail and be named failures, there is potential shame, a powerful effect of failure. Shame reconnects with dunce practices and has an archaeological history as well.

The word *shame* comes from a Teutonic root tied to infamous men and women, to disgrace. Interestingly, the *Oxford English Dictionary* notes no specific, earlier word root, although a pre-Teutonic origin means "to cover" or covering oneself.[20] Archaeologically, various trajectories of shame come out of Western thought: theological, philosophical, psychological (Broucek, 1991; Williams, 1993). The theological story begins with Adam's fall and the relationships of men and women and good and evil that follow. Failure, evil, and shame are interconnected in the Judeo-Christian psyche. The philosophical account comes out of Greek mythology and the responses of the likes of Plato and especially Aristotle. Further, the psychological version, much more contemporary, is a compelling tale from the Freudian tradition. More concretely, consider the impact of shame: The dunce wears the dunce cap on his head. The body/power attribution is strongly and externally evident. But consider also the interiorization of failure and what Foucault labels the "ethics" (and the histories) of repression of desire or of lack of autonomy.[21] In the ordinary language of failure, every teacher knows that "failure" is internalized so that individual students come to see themselves as failures.

Shame accompanies failure as well as the fear of failure that follows.[22] As indicated in a Foucauldian genealogical explanation, failure and the fear of failure produce and are produced by technologies of power external to the person. This power is "always already" there with the following relational characteristics: (1) co-extension with the network of the social body ("there are no spaces of primal liberty"); (2) interwovenness with other kinds of conditioned and conditioning relations such as kinship, sexuality, and production; (3) operation in multiple forms "that don't take the sole form of prohibition and punishment"; and (4) interconnection that delineates general conditions of domination, that is, as specific forms that are "organised into a more-or-less coherent and unitary strategic form . . . [but one not simply massive, primal, or binary]" (Foucault, 1977/1980a, pp. 141–142).

The effects of shame are powerful and, as indicated, are both direct and indirect. In both ways, to think of effect in its usual sense as connection to cause is misleading. According to Foucault's student, Giles Deleuze, power is everywhere. Further, this is "not because . . . [power] embraces everything, but because it comes from everywhere" (Deleuze, 1986/1988, p. 137). To come from everywhere, to just be everywhere, undermines notions of traditional power as controllable. Also altered in Foucault's understanding is power as a duality, as good in the hands of a humanist, autonomous individual or in similar collective terms, and as negative when used against humanist choice.[23] As shame exhibits, there is what might be called a double threat: Fear of shame conceals and leads to other concealments as protection against it. Doubling is then internalized as "self-discipline," what Foucault studies as ethics, as self-on-self subjugation. Subjugation is a formation of self, as part of a larger societal "system" of morality. The latter consists of the parts of ourselves subject to ethical judgment, the way in which the self is subject to judgment, the means by which we change ourselves in order to be ethical subjects, and the ideal to which we morally aspire (Davidson, 1986). All are integrated into memories of feelings of shame and of potential shame as produced by failure or potential failure. Importantly, as Hacking (1986) explains, Foucault's contribution is to claim that self "itself" is an artifact: "There is [not] any self, not any ego, any I" (p. 235). The artifactual-self "comes into being" through these ethical relations (and also the effects of powerful discursive practices and their environments). Ethics, while felt, is got at through language. But as Hacking (1986) also explains, "there is nothing private about this use of acquired words and practical techniques. The cunning of conscience and self-knowledge is to make it feel private" (p. 236). The dunce practice is just one example.

LANGUAGE ONCE MORE

Failure is actually sets of practices tied to language deeply entrenched in the world and within persons. Integral are such words as *dunce, laughter,* and *shame*—and each has various language manifestations that range from ordinary speech to disciplines of knowledge. The emphasis thus far has been on functions and effects of language; the following deals with its structures.

Linguistic structure, or the relations of words to themselves, also has an impact on failure, as one formulation has already illustrated. This is the changing nature of words such as *dunce.* Related is a change of context: Times change and the meanings of words change with them. Rorty (1989) admonished that "[we need to treat] . . . our language . . . as a product of time and chance" (pp. 20–21). Not only do words change by chance, but they also change by intent. Consider as examples the use of "Blacks" for African Americans, a term with more recently changed meaning. Or the distinctions drawn between *feminist* and *feminine* and what feminazi has done to *feminist* in the mid-1990s. Further, as is readily apparent, without contextual (historical, linguistic, and other cultural) clues and cues, one would not understand these words.

The ambiguous, tentative, and dispersed nature of communicative forms such as sentences also has an impact on failure. Prior to propositions and sentences, Foucault posits utterances/statements that he explains are repeated over and over and over: No fixed meaning is possible. If meaning is ambiguous, moreover, it is also tentative, both in its expressive and designative forms.[24] The latter is most striking: "Here is an apple." There are many varieties of apples; there are hybrid fruits that are apples/non-apples; there is "the apple of one's eye," and so on. As the linguistic structuralists generally proposed, there is no necessary correspondence between a signifier (a term) and its signified (what it means). Finally, deconstructionists have illustrated that word meaning is deferred: the covering of shame, the uncovering of shame on you, the biblical fear, and sexual innuendo; shame triggers all kinds of signifieds.[25]

This general nature of language is what might be called its openness, which is already part of common sense about communication and surely more than technicalities of linguistics. Moreover, not only are words used with openness, but some are open by function. Expressive language terms such as metaphors and canonical forms such as poetry convey this. Then there is the entire psychology of language use, as a Freudian influence, that is also taken for granted in everyday life. Freudian slips, unconscious memories, even self-delusion are accepted. Harking back to Taylor, all philosophers and historians such as Hacking—and especially Michel Foucault—have done is to add explanatory power to a late and postmodern preoccupation that we have with language.

ANOTHER SCENE

In a contemporary North American classroom, a well-meaning, overworked teacher responds to a recalcitrant student. To this point there have been hours of working through a lesson with seeming understanding—then a rupture. The teacher wants to throw up her hands in frustration. But she begins again even as she thinks, "Oh, my God, this child is such a dunce and I too am such a failure."

The teacher never calls her student a dunce; it would be cruel and unproductive. But she does want to intervene in the child's educational progress—on report cards, through parent conferences, perhaps in a special education faculty meeting, and even in a small one-on-one chat. She is familiar with failure; it is part of what she deals with every day. In Foucault's idiom, she takes part in a discursive practice, in ordinary language related to a larger vocabulary.

This discursive practice can be described as follows: School failure is a subset of a more general practice in Western life: to fail. The verb means to exhibit an insufficiency of some sort, a nonaction of something expected. School failure occurs in two "sites," persons and institutions: students, teachers, parents—people—either individually or collectively fail; the school, the family, the community—society and education—fail. Failure is not only defined against success but is so normed. There are traditions, conventions, and standards that set criteria for success and failure. One current convention to "assess failure" is the existence of nationally normed, standardized tests of literacy and numeracy (and other abilities and knowledges). When individual students, and the "attributive" social groups to which they belong are aggregated, there is a kind of abstract failure. For example, "minority males" in "inner city districts" fail—and these days these failures are put right on the front pages of the nation's newspapers. Every teacher believes that such "standardized failure" is internalized so that individual students come to see themselves as failures, a label confirmed again and again in classroom events. Teachers attempt to combat students' negative self-images, and one way of doing so is to seek causes and cures. Here, again, there is commonsense "rationalization"—finding fault for failure. "Impoverished homes," "uncaring parents," "overworked teachers," "impersonal schools" are all pointed to in turn.

This statement and the myriad others possible in similar situations illustrate the general idea of this chapter that life and language are one. Further, because of its ubiquity, the language of education—in this case of failure—is not something to be taken for granted. Paying attention to language is a first step toward intervention, toward educational change; further steps are to do something with what paying attention reveals.

The purpose of this chapter has been to offer a vision of the language of failure, of language in and for education, that alters how language, truth, knowledge, and action commonly are thought about. What is common but not naive is the idea that, as Rorty put it, "language is a mediator" of some deep sense that the "world has ways" and they need to be discovered and realized. With discovery and realization come typical beliefs about truth and knowledge and what can be done about the dunce situations in classrooms. But a vision of language from the likes of Wittgenstein, Davidson, Rorty, and especially Foucault tells something more: Language organizes, not just in constructions by an agent; in the language of this chapter, it has effects.[26]

The implication of the effects of language is that there is already in place a dangerous language of failure, potentially if not already in operation as a field of failurism. This is illustrated in historical dunce practices, in countless experiences of laughter and shame that they produce, and even in the everyday language by which failure is explicated. It is even more strongly and ironically manifested by this chapter and others in the present volume: As Foucault describes, no one knows to what ends it may be used. Thus questions remain: to name or not to name? From what kind of ethic may a caring and committed educator work? One central idea is that language itself changes and is potentially changed, along with its practices. However, even with change, language is not more than what it can be: ambiguous, tentative, and dispersed. Given their nature, once organized, discursive practices are difficult to change because they carry authority and authenticity—they seem true and right and thus good.

Foucault's insight is that language is not merely something beyond our control. Because it is all there is, it can be used as part and parcel of interventions—of attempts to change present situations. Importantly, all relations entail their own resistance to shifts. Part of intervention is that sometimes we recognize that "things are not right." If we are aware that much of the "construction" of what Foucault names "power/knowledge/subject" (who we are and how our worlds are organized) is indirect effect, that relations of discursive practices are tied to nondiscursive, environmentally linked forces that in turn constrain us externally and internally, then we work in and through language. We attempt to change these relations by first paying attention to their language—knowing that other relations also will be changed. Further, the bottom line is ethical: To do nothing means to accept the status quo—a language/practice/system of failure that really is ethically unacceptable. Furthermore, while Foucault might not put it this way, such intervention is "the hope we have" (see Rorty, 1982). To emphasize: It is indeed hope we have.

NOTES

The author thanks Brian Ellerbeck and Barry Franklin for the invitation to participate in this volume and for their invaluable editorial suggestions; Tom Popkewitz for ongoing conversation; and Laura Billings and Kathy Hytten for contributions to a previous version of this chapter.

1. *The Old Curiosity Shop* appeared as a serial in 1841–42 with illustrations by Cattermole and "Phiz." See the illustration, "The Dunce Improves the Occasion," in Dickens (1841/1951, pp. 188–189). Also, in 1842 Dickens journeyed to America. One of his letters concerns "A Smart Youngster," seemingly with a witty tongue, whom he met. See Slater (1978, pp. 91–92). One can only speculate about the transmission of the dunce symbol from England to America. There is mention in commentaries on Dickens of his popularity across the Atlantic. There is also the probability that schoolmasters transported the practice. See also Andrews (1972).

2. See Sternberg and Caruso (1985); Searle (1965/1986); McCarthy (1978) on Habermas; and Wittgenstein (1958/1986).

3. See especially the essays "Language and Human Nature" and "Theories of Meaning" in Taylor (1985).

4. See an earlier warning about educational conversation in Stone (1994).

5. The authority of language forms is not explicitly addressed here, but consider how much stock is placed in science, the canon, even an encyclopedia entry.

6. Foucault does not deny the possibility of direct human action but asserts that even as persons act, they do not know the "forces" these actions set in motion. To act, however, is always resistant and potentially provides the possibility of intervention for the better.

7. Jean-Francois Lyotard (1979/1984) calls large elements of world views, narratives and grand narratives; examples are capitalism and liberalism. See Rorty (1982, 1991) on Foucault.

8. While Rorty emphasizes the individual contributions of persons to practices, it seems to me that the other process occurs as well. Consider, for example, the change in language practices as a result of the modern women's movement.

9. Foundations are frameworks, sources, and starting and ending points as desired "certainties"; essentials are essences or formal universal properties; representations are correspondences between word and world. On essentialism in general, see Stone (1992); on representationalism, Rorty (1990).

10. For introductions to pragmatism and structuralism, see Murphy (1990), DeGeorge and DeGeorge (1972).

11. Again this is a reference to the idea of authority and power.

12. See Davidson (1984).

13. In this statement I have employed some phrases that are not Foucauldian but help to make sense of his notion of truth.

14. For assistance with research on dunces (there was almost nothing!), I want especially to thank Bernice Bergup of Davis Library, University of North Carolina–Chapel Hill. The remarks on etymology are drawn from the second edition of the *Oxford English Dictionary*.

15. As Hannah Tavares posits in her own Foucauldian study, these students and all others are in need of teacher "management." See Tavares (1996), and as well other recent educational studies in Marshall (1996), Hunter (1996), and Popkewitz (1991). Foucault (1975/1979) writes about surveillance and the disciplinary power of schools; see pp. 172–173, 175. Just as teacher management is "normal" today, Foucault's point is that by the eighteenth century, schools took on these typical functions.

16. See Arnold Davidson (1986) for an excellent account; also a more lengthy and technical account from Giles Deleuze (1986/1988).

17. Some poststructuralists call these traces, so embedded in the human psyche as to be sometimes almost unrememberable.

18. See Foucault (1963/1977b).

19. Failurism takes on the same ironic sense as Orientalism: One can imagine how a new educational specialty might be touted as a panacea for those "who have the disease." See Said (1986) on Foucault.

20. *Oxford English Dictionary*, 2nd ed.

21. For those who want to trace these roots, Foucault is part of the French tradition influenced by Freud and Heidegger.

22. Recall "the power" of societal groups that shame and ostracize.

23. Power for Foucault is a positivity; it both provides and punishes.

24. The reference here is to Taylor's (1985) theory that historically there are two language types, figurative and literal. Because of the tradition of representational language, the ambiguity of literal, ostensive language is more difficult to understand.

25. The writings of Jacques Derrida (1967/1991) are most significant here; see the excerpt from *Of Grammatology*.

26. See Popkewitz (1991), pp. 223ff.

REFERENCES

Andrews, M. (1972). Introduction. In C. Dickens, *The old curiosity shop* (pp. 11–31). Middlesex, England: Penguin Books.

Bristol, M. (1985). *Carnival and theater: Plebeian culture and the structure of authority in renaissance England*. New York: Methuen.

Broucek, K. (1991). *Shame and the self.* New York: Guilford.

Davidson, A. (1986). Archaeology, genealogy, ethics. In D. Hoy (Ed.), *Foucault: A critical reader* (pp. 221–233). Oxford: Basil Blackwell.

Davidson, D. (1984). *Inquiries into truth and interpretation.* Oxford: Oxford University Press.

DeGeorge, R., & DeGeorge, F. (Eds.). (1972). *The structuralists: From Marx to Levi-Strauss.* Garden City, NY: Anchor.

Deleuze, G. (1988). *Foucault.* Minneapolis: University of Minnesota Press. (Original work published 1986)

Derrida, J. (1991). *Of grammatology.* In P. Kamuf (Ed.), *A Derrida reader: Between the blinds* (pp. 31–58). New York: Columbia University Press. (Original work published 1967)

Dickens, C. (1951). *The old curiosity shop.* London: Oxford University Press. (Original work published 1841)

Foucault, M. (1972). *The archaeology of knowledge and the discourse on language* (A. S. Smith, Trans.). New York: Pantheon. (Original work published 1969)

Foucault, M. (1977a). History of systems of thought. In D. Bouchard (Ed.), *Language, counter-memory, practice: Selected essays and interviews* (pp. 199–204). Ithaca, NY: Cornell University Press. (Original work published 1970)

Foucault, M. (1977b). A Preface to transgression. In D. Bouchard (Ed.), *Language, counter-memory, practice: Selected essays and interviews* (pp. 29–52). Ithaca, NY: Cornell University Press. (Original work published 1963)

Foucault, M. (1979). *Discipline and punish: The birth of the prison.* New York: Vintage. (Original work published 1975)

Foucault, M. (1980a). Power and strategies. In C. Gordon (Ed.), *Power/knowledge: Selected interviews and other writings 1972–1977* (pp. 134–145). New York: Pantheon. (Original work published 1977)

Foucault, M. (1980b). Truth and power (C. Gordon, L. Marshall, J. Mepham, & K. Sopher, Trans.). In C. Gordon (Ed.), *Power/knowledge: Selected interviews and other writings 1972–1977* (pp. 109–133). New York: Pantheon. (Original work published 1977)

Foucault, M. (1980c). Two lectures. In C. Gordon (Ed.), *Power/knowledge: Selected interviews and other writings 1972–1977* (pp. 78–108). New York: Pantheon. (Original work published 1976)

Hacking, I. (1975). *What does language matter to philosophy?* Cambridge: Cambridge University Press.

Hacking, I. (1986). Self-improvement. In D. Hoy (Ed.), *Foucault: A critical reader* (pp. 235–240). Oxford: Basil Blackwell.

Hunter, I. (1996). Assembling the school. In A. B. T. Osborne & N. Rose (Eds.), *Foucault and political reason: Liberalism, neo-liberalism, and rationalities of government* (pp. 143–166). London and Chicago: UCL Press and University of Chicago Press.

Lyotard, J. (1984). *The postmodern condition: A report on knowledge* (A. S. Smith & B. Masumi, Trans.). Minneapolis: University of Minnesota Press. (Original work published 1979)

Marshall, J. (1996). *Michel Foucault: Personal autonomy and education.* Dordrecht: Kluwer.

McCarthy, T. (1978). *The critical theory of Jurgen Habermas.* Cambridge, MA: MIT Press.

Murphy, J. (1990). *Pragmatism: From Peirce to Davidson.* Boulder, CO: Westview.

Popkewitz, T. (1991). *A political sociology of educational reform: Power/knowledge in teaching, teacher education, and research.* New York: Teachers College Press.

Rorty, R. (1982). *Consequences of pragmatism: Essays, 1972–1980.* Minneapolis: University of Minnesota Press.

Rorty, R. (1989). *Contingency, irony, and solidarity.* Cambridge: Cambridge University Press.

Rorty, R. (1990). Introduction: Pragmatism as antirepresentationalism. In J. Murphy (Ed.), *Pragmatism: From Peirce to Davidson* (pp. 1–6). Boulder, CO: Westview.

Rorty, R. (1991). *Essays on Heidegger and others: Philosophical papers* (Vol. 2). Cambridge: Cambridge University Press.

Said, E. (1978). *Orientalism.* New York: Vintage.

Said, E. (1986). Foucault and the imagination of power. In D. Hoy (Ed.), *Foucault: A critical reader* (pp. 149–155). Oxford: Blackwell.

Searle, J. (1986). What is a speech act? In H. Adams & L. Searle (Eds.), *Critical theory since 1965* (pp. 60–78). Tallahassee: Florida State University Press. (Original work published 1965)

Slater, M. (Ed.). (1978). *Dickens on America and the Americans.* Austin: University of Texas Press.

Sternberg, R., & Caruso, D. (1985). Practical modes of knowing. In E. Eisner (Ed.), *Learning and teaching the ways of knowing.* Eighty-fourth Yearbook of the National Society for the Study of Education (pp. 133–158). Chicago: University of Chicago Press.

Stone, L. (1992). The essentialist tension in reflective teaching. In L. Valli (Ed.), *Reflective teacher education: Case studies and critiques* (pp. 198–211, 258–262). Albany: State University Press of New York.

Stone, L. (1994). Conversation in education: Empirical corrective or narcissistic pap? In A. Thompson (Ed.), *Philosophy of education: 1993* (pp. 278–285). Champaign: University of Illinois, Philosophy of Education Society.

Tavares, H. (1996). Classroom management and subjectivity: A genealogy of educational identities. *Educational Theory, 46*(2), 189–201.

Taylor, C. (1985). *Human agency and language: Philosophical papers* (Vol. I). Cambridge: Cambridge University Press.

Williams, B. (1993). *Shame and necessity.* Berkeley: University of California Press.

Wittgenstein, L. (1986). From philosophical investigations. In H. Adams & L. Searle (Eds.), *Critical theory since 1965* (pp. 767–788). Tallahassee: Florida State University Press. (Original work published 1958)

CHAPTER 2

Low-Achieving Children and Teacher Heroism: A Genealogical Examination

BARRY M. FRANKLIN

One of the most popular themes in our contemporary discourse on teaching low-achieving children is that of the heroic and valiant teacher. Often contrasted with his or her more conventionally minded colleagues, this teacher is depicted as one whose sentiments and attitudes render him or her a champion of the child. Heroic teachers typically are described as those whose affectional qualities manifest themselves in a respect for childhood, a dislike for bureaucratic rules and administrative authority, and an openness to curricular and pedagogical innovation.

Tales of teacher heroism have proved especially appealing to teacher educators in their efforts to prepare their students to work with such children. Using any of a number of recently written accounts and films, they introduce their students to supposedly heroic classroom teachers who are willing to take bold steps, often at risk to their own careers, to help low-achieving students, especially those who are Black and poor, succeed in school. Often pitted against them in many of these accounts are a larger number of timid and unresponsive teachers who see low-achieving children as burdens who merit neither their affection nor their support. The heroic teachers depicted in these books and films become for these teacher educators the models of progressive and innovative pedagogy that they hold out to their students.

Teacher educators, not surprisingly, differ about what it means to be a heroic teacher. Some have looked to a number of journalistic accounts (Fliegel & MacGuire, 1993; Freedman, 1990; Kidder, 1989) and to any of a number of recent and not so recent films (Dalton, 1995) that depict idealistic teachers who come to the aid of children in various states of crisis. The heroism of such individuals lies in their willingness to become involved in the lives of those they teach, to challenge their administrative superiors, and to change their curricular and instructional approaches to ensure the academic and personal success of their students. Others, however, embrace a more politicized notion of teacher heroism. They look to the so-called romantic critics of the 1960s (Herndon, 1968; Kohl, 1968; Kozol, 1967, 1991) and to the writings of radical, particularly neo-Marxist, educational scholars (Apple, 1982, 1986; Casey, 1993; Giroux, 1988; Giroux & McLaren, 1987). Heroic teachers, from this vantage point, not only seek to change existing school practices to ensure the well-being of children. They join with their students to try to change the political, social, and economic conditions outside of the schools that they believe breed low achievement. As one such educator notes, "outstanding teachers need to question the common sense—to break the rules to become political and activist in concert with the kids" (Ayers, 1994, p. 156). And of course there are still others whose conception of teacher heroism lies somewhere in between.

The past 10 or so years have seen a growing interest among educational historians in the history of teachers and teaching (Altenbaugh, 1992; Cuban, 1984; Herbst, 1989; Markowitz, 1993; Rousmaniere, 1994; Warren, 1989). These scholars have yet to chronicle the history of educating low-achieving children in America's public schools. Their research, however, has uncovered an array of information about the teaching of such children that can be gleaned from newspapers, school documents of one sort or another, and various archival material that informs us about teacher heroism. The most useful of these data describe the encounters of numerous twentieth-century classroom teachers with a diversity of low-achieving children. They take various forms, ranging from teacher reminiscences and secondhand accounts of teaching practices to school records and official reports. Such documents present a series of portraits that illustrate the various ways in which the public schools have made provisions for low-achieving children. In this chapter, I will undertake a genealogical examination of these accommodations and consider what that exploration tells us about the adequacy and usefulness of the notion of teacher heroism.

A GENEALOGY OF EDUCATING LOW ACHIEVERS

Lacking, as we do, a full history of educating low-achieving children, genealogy offers us a method of historical analysis for using the data that we do possess to explore the issue of teacher heroism. Devised by Michel Foucault from his reading of Frederick Nietzsche and expanded upon by numerous scholars of a poststructuralist persuasion, genealogy represents a departure from the traditional historiographical task of looking for the origins of past events and from those origins identifying their meaning and purpose. Genealogy instead involves writing a history of the present. The task of the genealogist is to identify certain important issues of the current moment, the teaching of low-achieving children, for example, and then to follow them back into the past. Genealogy is not, however, a form of presentism in which the historian writes about the past in terms of the present or attempts to locate present concerns in the past. Nor is it an approach designed to locate something of the present in the past and then to show how it followed a fixed and necessary pathway to the present. Using genealogy, we do not have to worry about locating the birth of the movement to educate low-achieving children. Nor do we have to worry about trying to figure out the ultimate meaning and purpose of this educational enterprise. We can begin instead by following over time the different and often discontinuous pathways that have been taken for educating such children. Examining these lines of descent will enable us to see the array of accomplishments, false starts, hesitations, and downright mistakes that have occurred as classroom teachers have encountered low-achieving children without worrying about the linkage, coherence, or consistency among them (Cook, 1993; Dreyfus & Rabinow, 1983; Foucault, 1977, 1980; Gutting, 1989; Mahon, 1992; Noujain, 1987; Toews, 1994).

Our genealogy of the education of low achievers in twentieth-century American schools identifies five lines of descent. One such line is represented by the special classes and schools that urban school systems established in the years around the turn of the twentieth century to accommodate handicapped children. Another line of descent is represented by efforts to introduce systematic curriculum or organizational modifications into regular classrooms as a means of providing for low-achieving students. A third pathway is the array of remedial programs, apart from special education, where low achievers could be temporarily placed until they acquired the skills and knowledge necessary to rejoin their peers in the regular classroom. A fourth route for educating low achievers can be seen in the informal efforts of individual teachers to help such children within their classrooms. A final element of this lineage is the compensatory educational initiatives that appeared on the scene from the mid-1950s onward to provide for supposedly culturally disadvantaged, minority youth. Exploring the lines of descent our genealogy has uncovered will provide us with a variety of vantage points from which to assess the adequacy of the notion of teacher heroism.

SPECIAL CLASSES AND TEACHERS' WORK

Late-nineteenth- and early-twentieth-century urban school administrators established special classes and schools for low achievers as a bureaucratic response to a school population that not only was growing in size but was becoming increasingly diverse in background, interest, inclination, and ability. Special classes and schools offered these school leaders new administrative capacities to accommodate the dislocations that this enrollment growth had brought. Of particular concern to these administrators was their belief that low-achieving children would interfere with the work of classroom teachers and the progress of their students. Special classes provided a way for public schools to accommodate these children while at the same time removing them from regular classrooms (Tropea, 1987).

School officials in Atlanta, Georgia, for example, began to contend with this problem as early as 1898. In January of that year, Superintendent William F. Slaton called on the city's Board of Education to adopt a regulation to "prevent children of dull minds and weak intellects from remaining 3 or 4 years in the same grade." As Slaton saw it, their presence in Atlanta's classrooms was leading "to the annoyance of the teacher and the detriment of the grade" (Atlanta Board of Education, January 6, 1898).

Atlanta's teachers evidently found the low-achieving children in their classes to be annoying and disruptive. At its October 1914 meeting, the Board of Education received a letter from J. E. Ellis, a teacher at Grant Park School, concerning one of her students, who had had, as she put it, an "epileptic fit." According to Ellis, Grant Park's principal, W. P. Davis, would not allow the child to return to class "because the presence of the child was liable to cause distraction in the exercise of the school." At the same meeting, the Board also received a letter from Belle Simpson, teacher of the deaf at Ashby Street School, requesting the removal of one Herbert Manning. In Simpson's words, "he disturbs the class by doing many unusual and unexpected things and continuously distracts the attention of the class and the work of the teacher" (Atlanta Board of Education, October 22, 1914).

During the first 2 decades of the twentieth century, Atlanta schools took a variety of steps to counter the disruptive influence of such children. In 1908, the Board changed the dismissal time of the city's first-grade classes from 2 p.m. to 1 p.m. to allow teachers in this grade to work with children in the other grades of the city's grammar schools who were behind in their studies. In 1914, the Board of Education authorized the establishment of summer vacation schools to enable students who had failed during the regular year to make up their work. A year later, the Board opened the city's first special class for mentally retarded children (Atlanta Board of Education, November 21, 1908, December 15, 1914, June 29, 1915). Within 5 years, the city would have seven special classes in its 44 grammar schools for White children and two special classes in its 15 Black grammar schools (Atlanta Public Schools, 1920–1930; Strayer & Engelhardt, 1921–22).

Atlanta was certainly not alone in establishing special classes. Known also as ungraded or opportunity classes, the establishment of these programs was a common response of school administrators at the turn of the twentieth century as they sought to cope with the increasing size and diversity of the school population. A 1931 U.S. Bureau of Education survey of 68 large city school systems reported that by the end of the 1920s 97% of these cities had established special classes for their lowest-achieving students, whom they variously labeled as mentally retarded or backward (U.S. Department of Interior, 1931).

Removing such children from regular classes no doubt brought some relief. As many teachers saw it, these children were difficult to teach and often troublesome to manage. As a consequence, working with them was seen as a time-consuming effort. What these low-achieving children required of teachers becomes apparent when we consider the experiences of special class teachers. In her reminiscences of her career in special education, Ann Covart, who began teaching in 1921 in St. Paul, Minnesota's special class for so-called "subnormal" children, recalled:

> We had to stay with our children all the time. We took them to the toilets. We ate with them at lunch, presumably to encourage good eating and manners. When school dismissed at 2:30 p.m., we were woofed. New students were sent to us anytime all year long. Not only did these children have learning problems, they had become discipline problems, because when you can't comprehend the lesson, you're inclined to do something else. (*A Collection of Memories*, 1960, p. 25)

Such responsibilities typically placed emotional burdens on special class teachers. Covart, for example, recalled her encounter with a colleague in the hallway:

> She was just coming up from there and was grinning ear to ear. That was unusual and I said to her "What are you laughing at? What is so funny?" She said, "Nothing, but if you don't laugh once in awhile, it'll get you." That remark changed my whole attitude. I had always been a worrier and an extremely sober person, feeling the weight of responsibility, insecurity, and being tense. I decided to try "to laugh it off" and I've been laughing ever since. Ha ha! Really, though, it saved me from a breakdown I'm sure because I had been taking things too seriously and felt as if I might fail. (*A Collection of Memories*, 1960, pp. 24–25)

Those who write about heroic teachers see such individuals as exerting extraordinary efforts on behalf of children. Heroic teachers, unlike their conventionally minded colleagues, are depicted as selflessly championing the cause of childhood, notwithstanding the risks to their professional careers or emotional health. Ann Covart's reminiscences clearly indicate that she cared about the children in her special class. Her remarks also suggest that her work was physically exhausting and posed risks to her mental well-being. Yet, it is difficult to say that her efforts were exceptional. From her vantage point, what she did for her special class children was simply part of her job as she saw it. She and her colleagues in St. Paul accepted the additional duties required of a teacher in a special class without fanfare as simply part of the job that they had assumed.

CURRICULUM MODIFICATION AND LOW-ACHIEVING CHILDREN

Creating special classes did not, however, free regular classroom teachers of their responsibilities for low-achieving children. There were children with less severe academic deficits who were not candidates for these special programs. In its 1933 report on handicapped children, the White House Conference on Child Health and Protection noted the diversity that characterized difficult-to-teach children. There were some with IQ scores up to the mid-80s whose low academic achievement and behavior problems required their removal from regular classrooms. There were, however, a host of other children who remained in regular classrooms but nonetheless required special help. These were children who, according to the White House Conference, had specific disabilities in "attention, memory, perception, or language" that were the result of such factors as illness, student–teacher conflict, or inadequate study skills. Such children did not need to be removed from regular classrooms. Rather, the Conference concluded that these low-achieving children for the most part should be provided assistance on an individualized basis within those classrooms (White House Conference on Child Health and Protection, 1933).

The suggestions advanced by the White House Conference represented a second path that urban school systems followed in providing for low-achieving children. Beginning in the 1930s, the Minneapolis Public Schools, for example, introduced a number of modifications in the regular school program as alternatives to special classes for educating so-called slow-learning children. Writing in March 1932 to the principal of the city's Bryant Junior High School, Assistant Superintendent Prudence Cutright suggested two such schemes. One involved a series of modified courses that were designed for children with learning problems. Although these courses would bear the same titles as regular junior high school offerings, they would be more applied and related to the day-to-day concerns of young adolescents. Social studies, for example, would be redesigned so that it would include content on community civics, and mathematics would be modified so that it would emphasize basic arithmetic skills.

A second scheme would place slow-learning junior high school students in regular classes for the first semester, during which time counselors would undertake an evaluation of each of these children. Based on the results of this study, an appropriate program would be designed for each of them for the second semester (Hardaker, 1932).

In 1933, Barbara Wright, Minneapolis's Supervisor of Counseling, in a letter to a New Orleans school board member identified several experiments that had been introduced to assist junior high school students who were experiencing academic difficulties. At Jordan Junior High School, all seventh- and eighth-grade students were being passed on to the next grade. Those who began exhibiting difficulties in the ninth grade were placed in a special group that was allowed to remain in this grade for three semesters instead of the usual two. At Lincoln Junior High School, seventh- and eighth-grade students who were experiencing problems were assigned for a half-day to a special teacher who provided instruction in the academic subjects, while remaining in their regular classes for homeroom, art, industrial arts, and physical education. And at Phillips Junior High School, the counselor conducted case studies of the entering children. Those identified as being below average were placed in low-ability groups that offered a modified curriculum (Cooley, 1933).

Minneapolis was not alone in introducing programs for slow-learning children. In September 1928, Detroit's Eastern High School created what was called the Special Grade Room for children who were intellectually normal but who were failing in their academic work. Such students, according to the teacher, Elizabeth Coolidge, either were not interested in school, could not function well in large classrooms, or had experienced any of a number of other factors that had interfered with their academic progress. Enrolling fewer children than other classes at Eastern, the Special Grade Room provided low-achieving students, Coolidge believed, with a less distracting environment and the chance for more individualized attention on the part of the teacher. The program, as Coolidge saw it, was quite successful. She noted that during its first year of operation, about 80% of the students assigned to the Special Grade Room were able to return to their regular classes (Coolidge, 1929).

Detroit's school administrators also undertook initiatives to keep low-achieving children in regular classrooms. In 1938, the city published a bulletin distributed to all homeroom teachers, describing ways in which they could provide for students who were "retarded" in reading. The bulletin offered an array of suggestions whereby homeroom teachers could work with their students who were having reading difficulties. They could, for example, enhance comprehension by providing students with questions to answer during their reading assignments. They could drill students on difficult words. Or they could teach students how to read silently. The bulletin recommended that homeroom teachers devote about 2 hours a week during the regular reading period to these remedial activities (Detroit Board of Education, 1938).

Similarly, New York City had an array of programs for low-achieving students. Within the city's junior high schools a number of remedial and "coaching" classes were established during the 1930s for students who had fallen behind in their work and needed individualized help (New York City Board of Education, 1935). In December 1934, the administration of Theodore Roosevelt High School opened its Reading School to provide remedial instruction for students with reading difficulties. A number of these children had entered Roosevelt while reading on the third- or fourth-grade level (New York City Board of Education, 1937). And with the assistance of the Works Progress Administration, the city had established remedial reading and arithmetic projects in more than 200 of its elementary schools (New York City Board of Education, 1939).

In February 1936, the Board of Education joined with Columbia University's Teachers College to establish Public School (P.S.) 500. Housed in the Speyer School Building at Teachers College, the school both provided programs for slow-learning and gifted students and served as a site for developing new curricula for these two groups of children (New York City Board of Education, 1936). The curriculum for slow learners was a modification of the activity program that was then being introduced in all of the city's elementary schools. Like its counterpart in regular classrooms, the Speyer School activity program shifted the organizing unit of the curriculum from the traditional disciplines of knowledge to daily life activities (New York City Board of Education, 1935, 1936).

One component of this program was a unit entitled "Public Services and Public Utilities." Two Speyer teachers, Martha Cook and Cele Brickman, developed the unit because their students seemed to know so little about how these agencies functioned. Cook noted, for example, that although her students were supposed to be in the fifth grade, a good number of them did not know how much it cost to mail a letter, how to dial a telephone number, what a gas meter was, or what the electric company did. The resulting curriculum used guest speakers, films, class discussion, and some reading material to familiarize children with the workings of such agencies as the post office, electric company, bank, and telephone company. During their study of the telephone company, the students viewed a film about the Bell Telephone Laboratories, visited a branch office of New York Telephone, listened to a talk by a telephone company representative, and toured the Museum of Science and Industry at Rockefeller Center. As part of the study, they wrote and illustrated their own book on telephones. Cook believed that the program provided the low-achieving children in her class with an improved understanding of the purpose and use of the public utilities they encountered in their daily lives. She reported that after the unit had been completed, one of her students was playing at a friend's house when his friend's mother had what appeared to be a heart attack. Realizing the seriousness of the situation, Cook's student remained calm, ran to a nearby drugstore, and telephoned for an ambulance. As a result, this woman was taken to the hospital in time to save her life (New York City Board of Education, 1938).

Students at Speyer School did not, however, simply study public utilities and related topics as ends in themselves. These topics evidently appealed to low-achieving students and kept their interest and attention. They served, then, as ideal vehicles whereby Cook and Brickman could introduce arithmetic, reading, spelling, and other traditional school subjects to low-achieving children (New York City Board of Education, 1938).

Contemporary discussions of teacher heroism make note of the fact that so-called heroic teachers routinely make adjustments in the curriculum to capture the interests of their students. Our portraits of Minneapolis, Detroit, and New York City indicate how important such modifications are in the teaching of low-achieving children. It was in fact the curriculum modifications of Speyer School that made it possible for Martha Cook and Cele Brickman to provide for their low-achieving students.

MINNEAPOLIS'S B CURRICULUM EXPERIMENT

Despite the seeming desire of urban school administrators to keep the least severely impaired of their low-achieving children in regular classrooms, it is not all that certain that teachers welcomed such students into their midst. This was particularly true for programs that, like the third pathway identified earlier for accommodating low achievers, temporarily placed such children in remedial settings outside of the regular classroom. The B Curriculum or Small Class Experiment introduced in the Minneapolis Public Schools during the 1940s is a case in point. In 1943, Minneapolis established a system of annual promotions to replace its existing practice of promoting students at the conclusion of each semester. As a consequence of this new policy, children in the secondary grades who failed a subject would have to repeat an entire year's work in that subject, not, as had been the case, a semester. Fearing that this change would increase failures among his less able students, Newton Hegel, principal of the city's Folwell Junior High School, devised a solution the following year that came to be known as the Small Class or B Curriculum Experiment. Selecting those seventh graders who he thought were most likely to receive failing grades, he assigned them to English, social studies, and mathematics classes with enrollments of about 20, which was half the size of the typical class at Folwell (Minneapolis Public Schools, 1949).

In introducing this program, Hegel at first thought that it would be necessary to modify the existing curriculum to reduce the failure rate among his students. He found, however, that extreme changes were not necessary. The reduced size enabled teachers to provide students with sufficient individual help to improve both their academic performance and their attitudes toward school. Some of these students, Hegel pointed out, improved sufficiently and were able to return to their regular classes. In order to allow those students who needed to remain longer in the Small Classes to do so, Hegel expanded the program first to the eighth grade and then to the ninth grade (Goslin, 1945).

In a report on the introduction of the B Curriculum, Eva Bergeland, Folwell's counselor, noted that the experiment necessitated only minimal changes in the school's curriculum. In English, B Curriculum students studied the same content as did students in the regular classes. In comparison to children in regular classes, however, these Small Class students used books written at a lower reading level, devoted more time to reading and spelling, and took more trips to the school library. In mathematics, the teachers spent more time than they did in regular classes on the fundamental operations, used simpler and more practical word problems, and took special pains to make their directions as clear and precise as possible. Despite these changes, Bergeland maintained, the teachers of Small Classes attempted to follow the regular curriculum as much as possible. She in fact argued that the introduction of extensive curricular modifications in the Small Classes would prove harmful to the students:

> Great care must be taken that children in the small classes do not feel inferior. The teachers must be optimistic and wholeheartedly a part of the program. Pupils placed in these classes must understand why they are placed there and also that there is no closed gate for them. They must understand that there is an open road into and out of the regular classes. No child should remain in the class against his will. The success of the B Curriculum program is found in the individual child's achievement, his feeling of satisfaction brought about by being "on his own," thinking independently and taking an active part in the life of the school. (Bergeland, 1945, pp. 5–6)

The teachers who were assigned to Small Classes when the program was introduced throughout the city's junior high schools in the fall of 1946 were not, however, as certain as were Hegel and Bergeland about the nature of this program. Some teachers, according to school system curriculum consultant Mary Beauchamp, did not see much difference between the Small Class Experiment and the regular school program and as a consequence supported it. Others, however, believed that the Small Class was "just a glorified special class" for less able students and tended to view the program with skepticism (Gilchrist, 1947).

The reports of junior high school principals about the implementation of the B Curriculum also suggest that teachers were divided in their assessment of this reform. Most teachers, according to these reports, indicated that introducing the B Curriculum was a relatively easy task requiring few, if any, changes in the regular program. Some Small Class teachers, however, according to these principals, made major modifications in their courses and in effect turned the B Curriculum into a remedial program. According to one of the principals, "no attempt [was] made to cover a definite course of study. Teachers have selected books and materials. [The] method of approach [was] adjusted to the groups." Another principal noted that teachers "have tried to pick and choose materials and topics suited to the abilities and interests of the groups." Finally, a third principal stated that his B Curriculum teachers used "different books" and assigned the students "easier projects" than did his regular class teachers (Gilchrist, 1946).

The problem was that Minneapolis's teachers had very different and often conflicting ideas of what the Small Class was all about. In March 1947, the B Curriculum Steering Committee met to hear reports from three of its subcommittees that were appointed to look at different aspects of the Small Class Experiment. Composed largely of classroom teachers, these subcommittees seemed hopelessly at odds concerning the purpose of this innovation. The report of the Subcommittee on Learning Materials noted that with some slight modifications, students in the Small Classes "should have the same curriculum as other students" (Minneapolis Public Schools, 1947c). The Policies Subcommittee, on the other hand, depicted the Small Class as a special class by describing it as "an adjustment program that will meet the needs of poor achievers such as students having poor work habits, mental and social maladjustments, physical or health handicaps, and language difficulties" (Minneapolis Public Schools, 1947d). Similarly, the Implications Subcommittee reinforced the difference between the B Curriculum and regular classes when it recommended that Small Class students be evaluated on the basis of their attitudes, not their subject matter achievement (Minneapolis Public Schools, 1947e).

In the face of these differing opinions about the Small Class Program, the city's school administration decided that beginning in the fall of 1947, it would discontinue the practice of placing such a program in each junior high school. Instead, it offered the principals four choices as to how they could accommodate slow learners. They could continue to offer the Small Class Experiment, place low achievers in selected regular classes with reduced enrollments, provide individualized tutorial assistance to slow learners, or leave it up to their teachers as to how to teach such students. Ten principals decided to continue with the Small Class Experiment. The other four, however, chose one of the other options (Minneapolis Public Schools, 1949).

With a variety of alternative provisions for low-achieving students in place, the school administration decided to evaluate the relative merits of these plans. During the 1947–48 academic year, all seventh-grade children who were enrolled in each of these four alternative programs were tested in reading, mathematics, and spelling; given a personality inventory; and assessed with a behavior rating scale. Not unexpectedly, the results were inconclusive. While some schools offering Small Classes reported that their students demonstrated academic growth, others reported no gains in achievement (Gilchrist, 1948; Minneapolis Public Schools, 1947a, 1947b, 1949).

In June 1948, the city's junior high school principals again were asked to choose which of the four plans for teaching low-achieving children they would adopt during the next academic year. This time, 11 of the principals indicated that they would abandon the Small Class Experiment, while only three decided to maintain the program (Gilchrist, 1948). Within a year the Small Classes would disappear from these three schools.

Some Minneapolis classroom teachers, it seems, saw the B Curriculum Experiment quite differently than did Newton Hegel. What Hegel envisioned in 1943 as a way to make Minneapolis's junior high schools more accessible to low-achieving children, became under the tutelage of some of the city's teachers separate and segregated classes. What Hegel saw as part of the regular school system, some Minneapolis junior high school teachers saw as a remedial program.

The literature on teacher heroism assumes that heroic teachers are different from other teachers. These discussions, however, say nothing about why and how these differences occur. Rather, the assumption seems to be that they are just there. Our discussion of the B Curriculum Experiment suggests that one important source for any of these differences may be the result of the background knowledge and preparation that teachers bring to their work. Those B Curriculum teachers who knew what Newton Hegel had in mind with his Small Class Experiment and consequently minimized the modifications they introduced, ended up as supporters of the program. On the other hand, those who confused the B Curriculum Experiment with a remedial or special education program became its opponents.

THE TEACHER SURVEY AT P.S. 45

Despite the seeming reluctance of some of Minneapolis's teachers to embrace the B Curriculum Experiment, we should not assume that classroom teachers uniformly rejected low-achieving children. The informal efforts of teachers to help such children within their own classrooms represents a fourth line of descent in the lineage of provisions that twentieth-century American schools have made for low-achieving children. In 1944, Angelo Patri, Principal of P.S. 45, a junior high school in the Bronx section of New York City, undertook a survey of his teachers' efforts with individual children during the year. He asked his teachers to complete a form in which they offered "a brief account . . . of some interesting developments in the character growth" of a child they had taught during the year. Teachers were asked to explain why they selected the particular child and to describe the steps they had taken to obtain "favorable results" (Patri, 1944).

Patri received about 100 responses to his survey. Almost uniformly the teachers who completed the survey indicated they wanted to help students who were having difficulties in their classes. In some instances, they placed low-achieving children in special programs of one sort or another. Miss Ryan, for example, reported that Howard O'Conner, an eighth-grade student, considered himself a failure. She noted that he came from a good home and was well behaved. Academically, however, he was a "slow learner." She had him reassigned to a "work-school program" in which he spent a half-day in a "slow class" for his academic work and the remainder of the day in a vocational program. As a result of this new assignment, according to Ryan, Howard's academic work improved and his absences decreased. As she put it, "his whole bearing has changed" (Patri, 1944).

In other cases, P.S. 45 teachers simply paid more attention and exhibited more concern for their difficult-to-teach children. Mrs. Keller noted that seventh grader Peter Mastropaolo did not do well academically. "Since he could not," she pointed out, "shine through his good work, he tried to get the attention of the class by his clowning and defiance." Her response was to talk to him about his misbehavior as well as to invite him to talk to her when he was bothered. "The fact that I listened to everything concerning him," she reported, "gave him a feeling of such importance that his desire to show off and demand attention disappeared entirely. He then did the best work that he was capable of doing" (Patri, 1944).

Another P.S. 45 teacher, Mr. Law, noted that Dominique Castiello, age 15, was "far below standard scholastically, apathetic, unambitious, [and] unmotivated." Although "firm and unyielding" in his application of classroom rules, Mr. Law made efforts to praise this student for whatever "small success" he attained. As a result, Dominique, according to Law, "commenced to develop an appreciation of, and a belief in his own ability" (Patri, 1944).

Not all P.S. 45 teachers succeeded in their efforts to improve the academic performance of their low-achieving students. Miss Holding talked about the "great amount of individual attention and time" that she had given to Dominick De Santis in hopes of overcoming his indifference to education. Yet, her report noted her "discouragement" over not being able to really help this child (Patri, 1944). Another teacher reported a similar sense of frustration in his dealings with Joseph Zito. He felt that the child should be able to do "better than average work" but was failing his class. Encouraging the child to do better seemed to lead to some temporary improvement but did not have "a lasting effect." He was "greatly disappointed" when toward the end of the term Joseph continued to exhibit his "extremely violent temper" (Patri, 1944).

At about the same time that Patri was conducting his survey, Josie Brennan was teaching low-achieving children in an adjustment class at Halsey Junior High School (P.S. 85) in Brooklyn, New York. As she reported in the school's staff newsletter, her students exhibited no initiative when it came to assembling their materials, were unable to ask appropriate questions, and could not complete the tasks that she assigned to them. In some instances, she found that dividing the class into smaller groups and having them work together to complete assignments helped. This seemed to be most effective for tasks that required students to construct some kind of physical object, such as a report or a manual. She did not find groupwork to be effective for teaching the language arts. "Here," she noted, "it was a case of 'blind leading the blind'." Other strategies that seemed to work for her were field trips, slide presentations, and radio programs. She reported that these approaches worked better in conveying information to her students than did written material. Finally, Brennan (1944) pointed out that in managing her pupils, concrete praise and rewards directed to individuals were more effective than offering "general" suggestions to the entire class.

Working with low-achieving children was for the teachers at P.S. 45 and for Josie Brennan something of a hit-and-miss proposition. Some things worked and others did not. There was, it seems, no one definitive way to instruct these children. Teachers who wanted to provide for difficult-to-teach students were forced to adopt a variety of approaches and hope that one or more of them worked. The determining factor, it seems, was luck. Some of these teachers were simply luckier than others in hitting upon a strategy or technique that proved successful in addressing the learning difficulties of a particular child.

Discussions of teacher heroism have virtually nothing to say about the role of luck in teaching. The assumption made in this literature is that the heroism of certain teachers can be explained by the attitudes that they display toward children. Yet, all of the teachers that Angelo Patri surveyed seemed to possess the sentiments that make for heroic teachers. So did Josie Brennan. Why, however, some of them were more successful than others in their work with low achievers seemed more than anything to be the result of serendipity.

LOW ACHIEVEMENT, MINORITY YOUTH, AND URBAN SCHOOLS

The encounters between teachers and low-achieving children that we have explored thus far in this chapter have occurred in big city school systems and for the most part took place as those schools attempted to accommodate growing numbers of children from poor and minority group families. In fact, throughout the twentieth century the problem of teaching low-achieving children has been intertwined with two particularly vexing and seemingly intractable difficulties of American urban schools. One involves the increasing racial isolation of Black and other minority children in city schools; the other involves the low educational attainment of these children.

During the 2 decades following World War II, these problems were accentuated by a number of economic and demographic changes in the nation's cities as a result of deindustrialization, suburbanization, and racial segregation. Virtually destroying the material prosperity and cultural health of the largest cities, these changes resulted in a system of urban public schools with an eroding tax base, a deteriorating physical plant, a disaffected teaching corps, and a largely African American and Latino student population, which was increasingly at risk of academic failure (Kantor & Brenzel, 1993; Rury, 1993).

In responding to these problems, urban school systems throughout the nation established an array of so-called compensatory programs, which represent the fifth and final element in our lineage of accommodations for low-achieving children. Illustrative of these initiatives were the attempts of Detroit and 13 other large city school systems during the 1950s to accommodate so-called "culturally deprived" children. Carl Beyerly, who headed the Detroit effort, described a host of different approaches that were then introduced at three of the city's junior high schools. Teachers in these schools, according to Beyerly, often appealed to children directly. In his words, they "try to show the child that someone is concerned about him." They talk to the child about the "advantage of staying in school." Other strategies included adapting reading material to fit the abilities and interests of disadvantaged children, using remedial or "coaching" teachers to help these children in reading, providing visiting teachers to work with the parents of such children, and establishing, at one school, a special ungraded class to offer disadvantaged students individual assistance. Other cities involved in the project introduced their own approaches. In Baltimore, school officials attempted to develop tests to assess the ability of disadvantaged students. Milwaukee established a number of so-called "orientation centers" throughout the city to place disadvantaged children in the schools that were most appropriate for them ("Schools Helping Underprivileged," 1959).

For many New Yorkers, particularly the city's African Americans and Latinos, the changing character of the city and its schools conveyed by the end of the 1950s a harsh and unpleasant reality. The schools they supported with their tax dollars provided an increasing proportion of the city's children with an education that was to their way of thinking inadequate and decidedly inferior to what suburban schools offered their White, middle-class clientele (Ravitch, 1974). In late November 1966, Rose Shapiro, a member of New York City's Board of Education and a community activist, reported to the Board about a meeting that she and Superintendent Bernard Donovan had had earlier that month with about 70 African American and Puerto Rican parents concerning the effectiveness of the city's schools. At the meeting the parents noted an array of problems that they saw as indicative of the inadequate education the city was offering to their children. At P.S. 158 in Brooklyn they reported that overcrowding had resulted in half-day sessions for first through fifth grades. Parents of children enrolled in Manhattan's P.S 194 complained that their children rarely were given homework and when they were, teachers never corrected it. At P.S. 123 in Manhattan, children were not allowed to take their textbooks home because there was not a sufficient number for the school's population. Children requiring remedial services at Brooklyn's P.S. 76, according to parents at that school, were placed on a waiting list. And at P.S. 133 in Manhattan, a teacher was reported by a parent to have stated that one of her students "has no brains" (Shapiro, 1966).

New York City's educational establishment certainly was not oblivious to such complaints. In the fall of 1964, the United Federation of Teachers, the Council of Supervisory Associations, and the Board of Education joined together to launch the More Effective Schools (MES) Program in 10 of the city's elementary schools. The Program included an array of innova-

tive changes in the city's schools designed to enhance the educational success of low-achieving youth, particularly minority group children (Rogers,
1968; Taft, 1974; "Union Backs 10 'Effective Schools,'" 1964). Included among
the changes were reductions in class sizes in the elementary schools to 22
children, heterogeneous grouping, lengthening the time that the school was
open from 3 p.m. until 6 p.m., the recruitment of enthusiastic and committed
teachers, and the provision for cluster teachers to assist regularly assigned
teachers ("Joint Planning Committee," 1964; "Nothing Less Will Work," 1963).

For many of the city's teachers, the MES Program was the vehicle through
which they were better able to provide for disadvantaged youth. Barbara
Shipley (1968), who taught in the MES Program at Manhattan's P.S. 146, in-
augurated a plan in 1968 to motivate her largely Black and Puerto Rican students by introducing them to well-educated and successful minority group
professionals. Exposing her students to such individuals, she reported, was
a "very positive approach to teaching racial pride and a positive self-image."
During the course of the year, she invited more than 20 visitors to her class,
including author Claude Brown, the Borough Presidents of the Bronx and
Manhattan, and Olympic athlete Thomas Randolph. For Shipley, these guests
were "a living symbol of what the child can be."

Shipley certainly did not believe that her program would cure the
problem of low achievement. Yet, it was an initiative that would offer her
children a positive view of the value of schooling:

> I will not say that all of my students are going to go to college. However,
> they now know this is a real live possibility for them, and hopefully, it will
> make the homework assignments tonight have a slightly higher rating than
> Batman. (Shipley, 1968, n.p.)

Shipley's efforts at P.S. 146 point to a factor that is central to discussions of
teacher heroism, namely, the role that insightful and innovative teaching
plays in helping children succeed in school. At the heart of Shipley's success was her understanding of how minority group professionals could
serve as role models for her students and her evident flair in devising a
teaching strategy that took advantage of the availability of such persons
in New York City.

LOW ACHIEVEMENT AND TEACHER HEROISM

Writing in one of his "Where We Stand" columns qua advertisements, the
late Albert Shanker commented on a cinematic effort to celebrate teacher
heroism, *Mr. Holland's Opus*. In the film, Mr. Holland, played by Richard
Dreyfuss, is a struggling musician with hopes of becoming a composer,

who is forced to become a high school music teacher to support his wife and soon-to-be-born son. At first resentful of his fate, Mr. Holland does little more than the minimum to keep his job. Gradually and somewhat grudgingly over the course of a 30-year career, he begins to exhibit a concern for the well-being of his students, which in turn leads him on the slow path of acquiring the attitudes, skills, and commitments of a heroic teacher. As Shanker (1996) sees it, the Mr. Holland of this film is very different from more typical renditions of teacher heroism:

> In the standard blackboard-jungle movie, an eager young teacher is thrown like fresh meat to the worst students in a tough school. A cynical senior teacher warns the new recruit not to "care" too much. After hair-raising confrontations attempting to reach the classroom thugs, the heroic teacher intervenes to help the toughest kid in a personal crisis; the class then rallies behind the teacher and they soon become the best students in the school. (p. 8)

Mr. Holland's Opus does not, according to Shanker, embrace what he believes to be this superficial and ultimately inaccurate view of teacher heroism. Shanker argues that the film conveys a more subtle understanding of what it means to be an exceptional teacher. Becoming such a person, Shanker points out, involves amassing just the right mix of affectional qualities, knowledge, and pedagogical skills to allow one to connect a given curriculum to the interests, abilities, and aspirations of one's students. Such an outcome, he goes on to say, is not easy or predictable. It is physically and emotionally exhausting work that proceeds, in Shanker's (1996) words, in "trial and error, intuitive" (p. 8) fashion over the course of an entire career. The encounters between classroom teachers and low-achieving children that we have thus far considered suggest the composition of these teacher attributes.

CONCLUSION

In this chapter, I have examined the theme of teacher heroism as it affects the education of low-achieving children. Establishing the genealogy of this educational enterprise yielded five pathways that twentieth-century public schools have followed in providing for low achievers. They are special classes, curriculum modifications, remedial programs, individual teacher initiatives, and compensatory programs. Looking at a series of portraits of encounters between classroom teachers and low-achieving children, each one illustrating one of these pathways, I identified a number of factors that affected the ability and willingness of teachers to make accommodations for low-achieving children.

One factor involved the beliefs that teachers held about what it meant to be a teacher. Ann Covart and her colleagues in St. Paul's special classes worked long and hard for low-achieving children because doing so represented their understanding of what teachers should do. A second factor had to do with efforts to modify the curriculum. What enabled Martha Cook and Cele Brickman at Speyer School to provide for their low-achieving children were their efforts to adapt the then popular activity program to the abilities and interests of their students.

Another important element affecting the interaction between teachers and low-achieving children was the background knowledge and preparation that teachers brought to their job. Looking at the B Curriculum Experiment, we saw that the opinions teachers had of this initiative depended on their understanding of its purposes. Teachers who recognized the goals of the program and resisted the temptation to water down their curriculum tended to welcome their assignment to one of the Small Classes. Those, on the other hand, who mistakenly confused the B Curriculum Experiment with a remedial program requiring a modified curriculum, turned out to be its opponents.

The efforts of teachers who took part in Angelo Patri's survey at P.S. 45 and the work of Jossie Brennan at Halsey Junior High School point to the role that a fourth ingredient, namely, luck, plays in the teaching of low-achieving children. In these two instances it appeared that teaching such children was at best a hit-and-miss affair. What ultimately seemed to determine the ability of teachers to accommodate difficult-to-teach children was their apparent good fortune in hitting upon a strategy that seemed to engage the particular students with whom they were working.

A fifth and final factor that we identified as influencing the encounters between teachers and low achievers was insightful teaching. Barbara Shipley, a teacher in one of New York City's More Effective Schools, was successful in her efforts with so-called culturally disadvantaged students because she was sufficiently perceptive to devise an engaging teaching strategy that held out high expectations for her students.

We should, of course, be cautious in trying to generalize about teacher heroism on the basis of our genealogy. In that vein, Hubert Dreyfus and Paul Rabinow (1983) warn us that

> For the genealogist there are not fixed essences, no underlying laws, no metaphysical finalities. Genealogy seeks out discontinuities where others found continuous development. It finds recurrences and play where others found progress and seriousness. It records the past of mankind to unmask the solemn hymns of progress. Genealogy avoids the search for depth. Instead, it seeks the surfaces of events, small details, minor shifts, and subtle contours. (p. 106)

Yet, the discontinuous paths for educating low-achieving children that our genealogy has uncovered do tell us something about the notion of teacher heroism. They suggest that such teaching is a far more complex effort than we heretofore have thought. Those whom we label as heroic teachers exhibit certain sentiments and affectional qualities that render them champions of childhood, foes of bureaucratic authority, and promoters of pedagogical innovation. But there is more to it than just having the right mental attitude. Heroic teachers possess a mix of attributes. Some are certainly affective in nature and involve beliefs about being a teacher. Others are more cognitive and have to do with teachers' background knowledge, the training they receive, their willingness and ability to modify the curriculum, and the astuteness of their pedagogical skills. And beyond all of this is serendipity. Heroic teachers are those who in the end are lucky enough to hit upon the right combination of affect, knowledge, and skill to promote the learning of particular children.

Teacher heroism certainly may be a popular notion in the discourse of teacher educators as they attempt to identify models of good pedagogy for low-achieving students. If, however, the concept is to prove useful in the education of prospective teachers, we will need a more nuanced understanding than we presently have of what it means to be a heroic teacher. Looking at the history of the education of low-achieving children provides us with a picture of what that deeper awareness entails.

NOTES

The research reported in this chapter was assisted in part by a grant from the Spencer Foundation. The data presented, the statements made, and the views expressed are solely the responsibility of the author. I am indebted to Kate Rousmaniere, David Labaree, and David Chawszczewski for their critical reading of earlier drafts of this chapter. Their comments and suggestions were especially helpful in sharpening my understanding of the notion of teacher heroism.

I am indebted to Kate Rousmaniere for sharing with me her copy of the teacher responses to Angelo Patri's survey at P.S. 45.

REFERENCES

Altenbaugh, R. J. (Ed.). (1992). *The teacher's voice: A social history of teaching in twentieth century America*. London: Falmer Press.

Apple, M. W. (1982). *Education and power*. Boston: Routledge & Kegan Paul.

Apple, M. W. (1986). *Teachers and texts: A political economy of classroom and gender relations in education*. New York: Routledge.

Atlanta Board of Education (1898–1915). *Minutes.* Atlanta Public School Archives (APSA).

Atlanta Public Schools (1920–1930). *School directory.* APSA.

Ayers, W. (1994). A teacher ain't nothin' but a hero: Teachers and teaching in film. In P. B. Bolotin Joseph & G. G. Burnaford (Eds.), *Images of schoolteachers in twentieth-century America: Paragons, polarities, complexities* (pp. 147–156). New York: St. Martin's Press.

Bergeland, E. (1945). Report of the B curriculum department. Minneapolis Board of Education Records, Special Education, Slow-Learning Pupils, B Curriculum Folder, Minnesota State Archives, Minnesota History Society (MBER).

Brennan, J. (1944). Problems of an adjustment class. *Halsey Clearing House,* 1, 6–7, James Marshall Papers, Box 3, Folder 25, Milbank Memorial Library, Teachers College, Columbia University.

Casey, K. (1993). *I answer with my life: Life histories of women teachers working for social change.* New York: Routledge.

A collection of memories from 1910–1960 as volunteered by St. Paul Educators. (1960).

Cook, D. (1993). *The subject finds a voice: Foucault's turn toward subjectivity.* New York: Peter Lang.

Cooley, E. (1933, May 5). Letter from Barbara Wright, Education, Slow-Learning Pupils, 1929–1964 Folder, Minneapolis Public Schools, Information Service Center (SLP).

Coolidge, E. (1929). Special grade room of Eastern high school. *Detroit Educational Bulletin,* 13(4), 6, Detroit Public School Archives, Professional Library, School Center Building, Detroit, Michigan (DEA).

Cuban, L. (1984). *How teachers taught: Constancy and change in American classrooms 1890–1980.* New York: Longman.

Dalton, M. M. (1995). The Hollywood curriculum: Who is the "good" teacher? *Curriculum Studies,* 3, 23–44.

Detroit Board of Education. (1938). *Causes of retardation in reading and methods of eliminating them.* DEA.

Dreyfus, H. L., & Rabinow, P. (1983). *Michel Foucault: Beyond structuralism and hermeneutics* (2nd ed.). Chicago: University of Chicago Press.

Fliegel, S., & MacGuire, J. (1993). *Miracle in East Harlem: The fight for choice in public education.* New York: Harper Perennial.

Foucault, M. (1977). Nietzsche, genealogy, history (D. Bouchard & S. Simon, Trans.). In D. Bouchard (Ed.), *Language, counter-memory, practice: Selected essays and interviews* (pp. 139–164). Ithaca, NY: Cornell University Press.

Foucault, M. (1980). Truth and power (C. Gordon, L. Marshall, J. Mepham, & K. Sopher, Trans.). In C. Gordon (Ed.), *Power/knowledge: Selected interviews and other writings 1972–1977* (pp. 109–133). New York: Pantheon. (Original work published 1977)

Freedman, S. G. (1990). *Small victories: The real world of a teacher, her students, and their high school.* New York: Harper Perennial.

Gilchrist, R. (1946, November 5). Letter from L. E. Leipold, T. O. Everson, & H. Tallakson. MBER.

Gilchrist, R. (1947, January 11). Letter from Mary Beauchamp. MBER.

Gilchrist, R. (1948, June 24). Letter from Mary Beauchamp. MBER.

Giroux, H. A. (1988). *Teachers as intellectuals: Toward a critical pedagogy of learning.* New York: Bergin & Garvey.

Giroux, H. A., & McLaren, P. (1987). Teacher education as a counterpublic sphere: Notes toward a redefinition. In T. Popkewitz (Ed.), *Critical studies in teacher education: Its folklore, theory and practice* (pp. 266–297). London: Falmer Press.

Goslin, W. (1945, May 14). Letter from Newton Hegel. MBER.

Gutting, G. (1989). *Michel Foucault's archaeology of scientific reason.* New York: Cambridge University Press.

Hardaker, E. J. (1932, March 18). Letter from Prudence Cutright. SLP.

Herbst, J. (1989). *And sadly teach: Teacher education and professionalization in American culture.* Madison: University of Wisconsin Press.

Herndon, J. (1968). *The way it spozed to be.* New York: Simon & Schuster.

Joint planning committee for more effective schools. (1964, June 4). *United Teacher,* United Teacher Records, United Federation of Teachers Collection, Box 2, Wagner Labor Archives, Elmer Holmes Bobst Library, New York University (UT).

Kantor, H., & Brenzel, B. (1993). Urban education and the "truly disadvantaged": The historical roots of the contemporary crisis, 1945–1990. In M. Katz (Ed.), *The "underclass" debate: Views from history* (pp. 366–402). Princeton: Princeton University Press.

Kidder, T. (1989). *Among school children.* Boston: Houghton Mifflin.

Kohl, H. (1968). *36 children.* New York: Signet Books.

Kozol, J. (1967). *Death at an early age: The destruction of the hearts and minds of Negro children in the Boston public schools.* Boston: Houghton Mifflin.

Kozol, J. (1991). *Savage inequalities.* New York: Crown.

Mahon, M. (1992). *Foucault's Nietzchean genealogy: Truth, power, and the subject.* Albany: State University of New York Press.

Markowitz, R. J. (1993). *My daughter, the teacher: Jewish teachers in the New York City schools.* New Brunswick, NJ: Rutgers University Press.

Minneapolis Public Schools. (1947a). Evaluation committee. MBER.

Minneapolis Public Schools. (1947b). Proposed evaluation of small class plans. MBER.

Minneapolis Public Schools. (1947c). Recommendations of the subcommittee on learning materials. MBER.

Minneapolis Public Schools. (1947d). Report of the policies subcommittee of the B curriculum steering committee. MBER.

Minneapolis Public Schools. (1947e). Report of the subcommittee on implications for the curriculum in general. MBER.

Minneapolis Public Schools. (1949). Report of the small class or B curriculum experiment. MBER.

New York City Board of Education. (1935). *All the children: Thirty-seventh annual report of the superintendent of schools.* New York City Board of Education Archives, Milbank Memorial Library, Teachers College, Columbia University (NYC).

New York City Board of Education. (1936). *All the children: Thirty-eighth annual report of the superintendent of schools.* NYC.

New York City Board of Education. (1937). *All the children: Thirty-ninth annual report of the superintendent of schools.* NYC.

New York City Board of Education. (1938). *Public service and public utilities.* NYC.

New York City Board of Education. (1939). *All the children: Forty-first report of the superintendent of schools.* NYC

Nothing less will work . . . now is the time. (1963, April). *United Teacher*, Box 1, UT.

Noujain, E. G. (1987). History as genealogy: An exploration of Foucault's approach to history. In A. Phillips Griffiths (Ed.), *Contemporary French philosophy* (pp. 157–174). Cambridge: Cambridge University Press.

Patri, A. (1944). Survey of teachers, Angelo Patri Papers, Box 87, Library of Congress, Manuscript Division, Washington, DC.

Ravitch, D. (1974). *The great school wars: New York City, 1805–1973.* New York: Basic Books.

Rogers, D. (1968). *110 Livingston Street: Politics and bureaucracy in the New York City school system.* New York: Random House.

Rousmaniere, K. (1994). Losing patience and staying professional: Women teachers and the problem of classroom discipline in New York City in the 1920s. *History of Education Quarterly, 34,* 49–68.

Rury, J. L. (1993). The changing social context of urban education: A national perspective. In J. L. Rury & F. A. Cassell (Eds.), *Seeds of crisis: Public schooling in Milwaukee since 1920* (pp. 10–41). Madison: University of Wisconsin Press.

Schools helping underprivileged to adjust to life. (1959, October 10). *Detroit News*, Norman Drachler Papers, Box 57, The Paul and Jean Hanna Archival Collection, Hoover Institution, Stanford University, Stanford.

Shanker, A. (1996, February 19). Where we stand: Truths about teaching. *New Republic*, p. 8.

Shapiro, R. (1966, November 28). Memorandum from Rose Shapiro, Rose Shapiro Papers, Box 7, Folder 7, Milbank Memorial Library, Teachers College, Columbia University.

Shipley, B. (1968, May 29). Development of every child to the uttermost limits. *United Teacher*, Box 3, UT.

Strayer, G. D., & Engelhardt, N. L. (1921–22). *Report of the survey of the public school system of Atlanta, Georgia* (Vol. 1). New York: Teachers College.

Taft, P. (1974). *United they teach: The story of the United Federation of Teachers.* Los Angeles: Nash.

Toews, J. E. (1994). Foucault and the Freudian subject: Archaeology, genealogy, and historicization of psychoanalysis. In J. Goldstein (Ed.), *Foucault and the writing of history* (pp. 116–134). Oxford: Blackwell.

Tropea, J. (1987). Bureaucratic order and special children: Urban schools, 1890s–1940s. *History of Education Quarterly, 27,* 29–53.

Union backs 10 "effective schools" (1964, September 15). *United Teacher*, Box 2, UT.

U.S. Department of Interior. (1931). *Public school education for atypical children.* Washington, DC: U.S. Government Printing Office.

Warren, D. (Ed.). (1989). *American teachers: Histories of a profession at work.* New York: Macmillan.

White House Conference on Child Health and Protection. (1933). *The handicapped child: Report of the committee on physically and mentally handicapped.* New York: Century.

CHAPTER 3

"Some Teachers Are Ignorant": Teachers and Teaching Through Urban School Leavers' Eyes

RICHARD J. ALTENBAUGH

In my physics class, we were doing an experiment, and I was having problems with my lab partner 'cause my partner was never there. I went to the
teacher and asked him a question. Another student was in front asking a
question also. He helped that student, and I went to ask my question again
and he liked skipped over me and went to this White girl. She was really
smart and she always did her work. He like helped her. . . . I felt like, well I
was doing the best that I can being that I was by myself. . . . That one teacher
I felt it all the time. . . . A lot of times with other teachers it was more subtle.
Like if they would see you in the hall they would ask you for a pass. If they
would see a White student walking past they might say, "Keep on walking."
                                          —Interview with urban school leaver

This chapter captures how urban school leavers perceived teachers. Relying on transcribed, in-depth interviews of 100 informants at the Pittsburgh
Job Corps Center, which were conducted between 1986 and 1994, it reconstructs their classroom experiences. These narrators are, according to the
literature, known as dropbacks, that is, students who left school then re-
entered in an educational program to complete their Graduate Equivalency
Diploma (GED). This is a relatively overlooked group. Yet their experiences
reveal a dynamic school leaving process. According to estimates, approxi-

mately 10 to 38% of all school leavers return, and 90% of them continue their education onto postsecondary levels (Altenbaugh, Engel, & Martin, 1995).

Rather than describe what narrators said, this chapter allows them, as much as possible, to speak for themselves and for other school leavers. It preserves their language and speech patterns, because, as Spradley (1979) stresses, language is "a tool for constructing reality" (p. 17). This chapter begins with a brief overview of the Pittsburgh Public School District; moves to a short description of the informants; focuses on their perceptions of teachers, teaching, and the formal curriculum; and concludes with a brief discussion of classroom relationships between teachers and eventual dropouts. This chapter relies on more than mere descriptive narrative, since it analyzes dropback recollections within the context of school leaver literature as well as historical experience and social theory. Finally, whenever possible, this chapter uses the term *school leaver* rather than dropout. First, this represents an all-encompassing label, which includes dropping out, pushing out, fading out, easing out, as well as combinations of these various school leaving experiences. Second, the term *school leaver* avoids negative, almost pathological connotations associated with the term *dropout*, which implies that something is wrong with the individual. This study does not cast school leavers as helpless victims, but stresses human agency; these narrators chose to abandon their schooling based on the conditions they faced (Altenbaugh, Engel, & Martin, 1995).

PITTSBURGH PUBLIC SCHOOLS

The Pittsburgh school system consists of 53 elementary (grades K–5), 14 middle (grades 6–8), and 11 high (grades 9–12) schools, and maintains a magnet school program. During the 1992–93 school year, 40,413 students attended the city's schools; African Americans constituted 21,266, or 52.6% of that total. The high schools claimed a total of 11,349 students, with 5,427, or 47.8%, African American.

Pittsburgh's 11 high schools maintained an average enrollment of 946 students each during the 1992–93 school year. Size ranged from 303 students at Letsche, the district's alternative school, to 1,436 at Allderdice, with six claiming over 1,000 students each year. While Pittsburgh relies on large high school buildings, it keeps its class size small, averaging 18.7 students. This figure encompasses several categories that reflect a broad spectrum of subject areas. Academic courses, like English, social studies, and so forth, host 21.0 students each, while nonacademic classes, such as music and physical education, typically enroll 24.2 students. Vocational subjects, such as business education and home economics, accommodate 14.5 students, and gifted and special education courses maintain the smallest number, with 13.9 and 6.8 students, respectively. In spite of this modest average class size, informants claimed that they attended large classes. Why did they perceive this? As we will see, traditional teacher pedagogy, with desks lined up in rows, de-emphasized individual and small-group learning. Narrators disliked this impersonal approach. It further interfered with their recollections of relatively small class size. That is, instructors implemented a teacher-centered, whole-class approach, leaving students with the impression of large classes; teachers simply did not take advantage of small classes to alter their pedagogy.

A correlation exists between school size and school leaving, particularly for minority students (Bennett & LeCompte, 1990). Stoughton and Grady (1978), in their Arizona study, found the following startling data: "The highest dropout rate occurred in schools with student enrollments of 1000–1500 students. . . . In small schools with up to 200 enrollment the dropout rate was half the overall annual rate in Arizona" (p. 314). Small school buildings in their investigation remained flexible, fostered a more personal relationship between teachers and students, and appeared more committed to nurturing students.

The Pittsburgh school district officially defines a *dropout* as "a pupil who leaves school for any reason except death, before graduation or completion of a program of studies without transferring to another school or educational program." This district therefore excludes from its school leaver figures school-age students who enter federal programs like the Job Corps and correctional institutions, or those who return to school. It collects and analyzes school leaver data based on 4-year cumulative and annual percentages. The cumulative school leaver rate since 1983 has averaged 24.7%, ranging from 28.4 to 18.2%. The annual rates have averaged 6.9%, with a low of 6.0% in 1987–88 and a high of 7.6 in 1988–89. Sharp disparities also exist between buildings. The annual school leaver rates for high schools during the 1992–93 school year ranged from 1.1% at Perry Traditional Academy to 16.0% at Letsche Education Center. This can be misleading, however. Some highly rigorous programs, like that at Perry, can transfer students back to their home institutions or to alternative schools, like Letsche, to mask their school leaver rates.

Pittsburgh students typically abandon school sometime during the tenth grade at age 17. Race plays a major role, since African Americans leave school at a higher rate than any other group. With a 7.0% school leaver rate district-wide in 1992–93, African American males and females left school at rates of 9.6 and 7.3%, respectively. Rates for "other" male and female school leavers were 7.0 and 4.5%.[1] How did they perceive teachers, teaching, and the formal curriculum?

INFORMANTS

The narrators represented every high school, as well as two middle schools, in the Pittsburgh Public School District; thus, the interviews provided a systemic overview. Most of the informants, in many ways, fit the image of the stereotypical school leaver. They were predominantly minority students and came largely from nontraditional households. African Americans constituted 85% of the interviewees, outstripping the proportion of African Americans in the district's schools. The interviews included only two immigrants: one from Italy and another from Trinidad. Females represented 59% of the 100 narrators, exceeding the district's figure. African American women constituted 49% of the sample. Ages ranged from 16 to 23 years; the mean age was 18.56 years, and the mode was 19. The ages indicated that their school experiences were very recent. Some indicated that they had abandoned school only weeks before; most were within months of having left. Very few, especially those in their twenties, had been out of school for a few years.

Regardless of race and location, socioeconomic background has been directly correlated to school leaver rates (Beck & Muia, 1980). During the 1992–93 school year, 38.6% of the student population in the Pittsburgh schools received public assistance. The district, using information from the Department of Public Welfare, decides which students are eligible for free and reduced price lunches based on family income. While 62.3% qualified for this benefit that year, only 25.1% overall actually applied for it, and only 16% of high school students used the free and reduced lunch option. More students, according to school district data, have been applying for this benefit each year.[2]

Judging from their parents' or guardians' occupations—domestics, nurses, construction workers, security guards—or their unemployed status, and from the family's place of residence, in the Hill District, Homewood, or Garfield sections of Pittsburgh, narrators came mainly from poor, or at best working-class, families and communities, primarily African American sections of the city. To make matters worse, 50% of the informants indicated that their parents or guardians were unemployed or collecting welfare or a pension. The interviews failed to determine whether those in the employed cohort were working full time; many of them were likely underemployed, laboring either at part-time jobs or irregular employment, such as construction work. Moreover, even full-time work is often poorly paid.

These school leavers, therefore, came from economically distressed families. This profile fits with national patterns and reinforces the correlation with minority status: "In 1987, about 40 percent of Black and Hispanic children were living in families with incomes below the poverty level, compared to 25 percent for White children" (Rumberger, 1991, p. 73).

TEACHERS AND TEACHING

The subject of teachers generated strong responses and demonstrated the critical role that teachers and their classroom practices play in the lives and decision making of school leavers. As one female narrator summarized it, some teachers are "real nice," but "some teachers are ignorant." Teachers simply represented the best and the worst of schooling for these informants; instructors even shaped narrators' most and least favorite subjects.

Students sorted teachers according to surprisingly simple criteria; race appeared to mean little, but caring and pedagogical skill were meaningful. Caring, a subjective or affective element, implied selfless, egalitarian, and consistent treatment of all students. One African American female informant easily and clearly described a caring teacher: "Someone who takes time and who sits down and helps you when you need their help and who will give you their attention that you need. . . . Two that I can really remember; that really stuck out at the time." She described poor instructors as "teachers that really did not care, who have the time to spare but is not willing to give the time to you. I had a lot of them." Through many interviews, caring for students appeared to be centered consistently on two basic elements, sharing time and exercising patience. Narrators appreciated those seemingly selfless classroom instructors who, devoted to a nurturing process, freely gave their time reviewing or reteaching information. These were too few. Other studies confirm this finding. Nationwide, a mere 6% of potential school leavers view their teachers as "friends" (Beck & Muia, 1980, p. 69).

This became patently clear in one particular case. A tenth-grade African American female had missed a great deal of school because she had a child at home: "Half the time I couldn't find nobody to watch her." Her daughter was "too young" for a child care center. This set the stage for a confrontation with a teacher, which led to her suspension:

> I was failing the class and [the teacher] told me to do a report [and] he would pass me. I would just pass with a C. So I said all right, and I did a 15-page report. It took me about 2 weeks, but I did it. And when I handed in my report, and I came back 3 days later for it, to see what I had got, he told me he lost it. And I just went off. I started throwing books and chairs at him.

She appealed to the school's dean: "I told the dean. He said that he can't do nothing about it." She believed that the system and personnel were unjust. She also felt alienated from the personnel. Between ninth and tenth grades, she had attended three different high schools, causing her to observe: "I didn't really know my teachers." To add insult to injury, she did not receive word of the suspension until after she left school. "That day, when I went home, it was the last period of the day, they had already called my mother and told my mother don't send me back. They sent a letter saying I was kicked out."

Some Pittsburgh narrators reconstructed classroom routines in detail. One female student provided a thoughtful, balanced, and sensitive view, first briefly describing two "good" instructors, and then quickly moving to her experiences with a "poor" teacher:

> I liked my gym teacher and my music teacher. Those classes were interesting. The teacher took time with you. She didn't rush you into things you didn't want to do. [Other teachers] just throw a paper in your face and say do it. Whereas some students may not be on the same level as other students. And they just . . . sometimes they just don't take the time out. Like everybody is on the same level.

She proceeded to recreate this latter process through a description of her U.S. history course: "I used to like history. In about the ninth grade, I used to like history, but when I got to the tenth and eleventh grade, it got kinda hard. Really hard. It didn't seem like I had the interest in it like I did when I was in the ninth grade or anything." Her observations pointed directly to the teacher, not the subject matter: "You know when he talked to us it was really fast and it just seemed like the class . . . I don't know . . . everything was on the same speed, but I wasn't. What he was talking to them, I hardly understood. It seemed he was talking Chinese or something." This, coupled with the size of the class, intimidated her:

> And then the class was so big. We had about 25 or 26 people. I really felt like they really think I was dumb. But I'm not. I never really asked him things. 'Cause the class seemed too big, I would have never been like the only one who raised my hand. . . . What I'm saying is that he is only one person. In a big class, like you can't just sit there and tutor one child.

The informant, at this point, ignored the interviewer, who had commented that the class size she described was average, perhaps modest in some cases, and persisted with her recollection, focusing on the instructor and the total absence of class discussions: "What he said, was said. Then the kids would get to their papers and do their book work. I probably would catch up with the book work. And when it came to him telling us, like a filmstrip we just seen, maybe giving us some background on that, it was crazy the way he talked, real fast." She avoided going to the teacher for help: "Sometimes my older sister would help me, cause she would take the same class but different periods. She made me have a little clearer look at it, but by that time I was lost."

When the interviewer asked whether teachers seemed to care, this student was unequivocal: "They could care less if you studied or not. They were just getting paid. That's what they were saying to us. Yeah, a couple of teachers told us: 'I'm getting paid, so if you want to sit there and joke around, I'm still gonna get my check.' That's what they said." This narrator perceptively recognized and grappled with a contradiction here, first noting the idealism that originally spurred most teachers to enter the classroom: "Some of them had a nice thought about kids. For them to be a teacher, they have to have some kind of interest in the child, right? They want to give something to the child that they never had. Some are like that and some of them say that they are there for the pay." She then attempted to explain such teacher burnout—albeit in vague terms: "I have to admit that they go through a lot of hell." But she quickly returned to a critical perspective, offering insight into the harmful consequences of irresponsible teacher comments: "If teachers say that to a student . . . you say, 'Wow.' Why he say that? That makes a student want to leave."

Many informants also recalled favoritism. One narrator described a humiliating experience for many students:

> Every time after a test . . . she would pass out the tests and read out your scores. The perfect students would be read off first, and there would be like three A's in the class, everybody else are D's and failed. I guess the teacher did that to make the people embarrassed to make them try harder.

Students either resented it or appeared resigned: "All teachers have their favorites. I think so. But there is one teacher . . . that don't though. She treats everybody the same. That is what she should do. Some teachers, if they don't like the students they show it." One female student observed how teachers chose favorites:

> Most of the kids that were real smart in class. The other ones, they just ignored altogether. They was always nicer to those [smart] students and always mean to the others. They would like, if a kid missed a day of notes, he would give it to him and help him out, but he wouldn't the other students.

Another student stoically responded: "It didn't bother me." Kelly's (1993) interviews of California continuation school students find similar treatment based on academic achievement and ability. An African American male recognized differential treatment given to students according to academic ability and career goal. The "scholars program" stresses an intensive approach to academic work, and students enrolled in it appeared to receive preferential treatment by everyone: "If you were a scholar, you were somebody. They went on a lot of field trips, the scholars. They used to go on the bus everyday" (p. 105).

Favoritism occasionally encompassed racism. Most informants failed to describe social or systemic racism, but many pointed to individual racism, complaining about biased teachers and administrators. An African American male drew a direct connection between staff racism and his decision to leave school: "That's one of the main reasons I dropped out of school, because of the racial problem with the teacher." He never elaborated on his comment. However, for him, race mattered in American society, "because some jobs they judge you by your color. You can't live in certain cities or towns. When you are the only Black or White person in town, you will have problems." A White male student, like other narrators, denied that outright racism existed, but his comments implied racial tensions: "There is a lot of people who are still prejudiced against Blacks. And there's a lot of Black people who think all White people are prejudiced."

Individual racism confronted one African American male student. His recollection of racism emerged indirectly from a question about field trips; he pointed to a trip he and 15 classmates had taken to Howard and Tuskegee Universities on a charter bus. He observed that they visited only those two schools "cause all the students were Afro-American." He disagreed with this strategy: "I felt that we were in [Washington,] D.C., and there were like George Washington University, Georgetown, and American Universities. There was like three or four other universities that we could have seen, but we didn't. We just went to Howard and we just went to Tuskegee." He then described the selection process by which the students voted to visit these particular institutions: "There was a meeting and the students decided where they wanted to go. But, of course, all the students want to go to Howard, because everybody knows about Howard. They hear about how much fun it is. I felt it shouldn't have been up to the students, because of a lot of things we don't know." This narrator strongly objected to this procedure: It disturbed him that neither teachers nor counselors, who served as sponsors and chaperons, offered any other options to these African American students except traditionally African American institutions.

Pedagogical practice represented a more observable and less subjective measure of teacher effectiveness, and students maintained a critical and perceptive eye concerning the classroom routine. School leavers too often recalled: "Some [teachers] don't care if students learn." Teachers, concerned only with control, combined discipline with pedagogy, as in the case of one 16-year-old school leaver: "You would be in class and they would give you an assignment or something. If the class is disruptive, they would give you a test on it, and expect you to pass it in a few minutes!" The failing grade assuredly received through this process served at best as a lesson about behavior, and at worst as punishment, giving the students what they deserved because they were off-task. However, not all informants criticized this dreary classroom environment. One student saw social studies as "fun" because, as he stated it, "all we did was dittos and look the answers up in the book. And we got good grades." This narrator appreciated his teacher's lack of intellectual challenge, as long as he received a "just" reward. Whatever the case, students grew detached and felt unchallenged.

Cynical and calloused teachers reinforced another African American male's alienation: "To me the difference as far as the teachers was concerned, was that they sort of had an 'I don't care' attitude. Get you in and get you out. Just so long as you get that D." This narrator pointed to only one exception, a music instructor: "He was a good teacher, because he was very concerned about what you were doing. He wanted to make sure that you were doing good in all your classes. He was good. He knew that I was having problems, and he tried to encourage me." Otherwise, he thoroughly disliked his courses:

> On a daily basis, one of my classes, everyone would come in and it would take the teacher 20 minutes to get everybody quiet. And finally they all would start doing their work. You weren't taught anything. . . . You went step-by-step with the book. They had like booklets that you would do. By the middle of the class all of a sudden somebody would try to distract the class. Then he or she would get into it and they would curse out the teacher and walk out. And then by that time everybody is laughing and talking and the class is disrupted. And then you just get everyone not doing anything but talking and socializing. By that time, it's time to go.

He related this directly to obstreperous peers and a drudge-like classroom routine.

This pedagogical experience is not new. Cuban (1984) argues that secondary teachers have not altered their teaching methods profoundly since the late nineteenth century, "despite intense reform efforts to move class-room practices toward instruction that was more student-centered" (p. 2). In learner-centered classrooms, students have opportunities to talk as much as, if not more than, the teachers. Students often work individually or in small groups, seldom as a whole class. Students also assume a great deal of responsibility for selecting and organizing the content, as well as creating and enforcing classroom rules and procedures. In addition, learner-centered classrooms contain a variety of instructional materials and resources, to which students have access at least half of the time. Finally, classroom desks and other furniture appear to be arranged to facilitate individual or small-group work (Cuban, 1984).

This setting sharply contrasts with teacher-centered classrooms that Pittsburgh school leavers consistently described. Teacher talk dominated the time, usually during whole-class sessions, with the desks arranged in the traditional rows facing the teacher, the teacher's desk, and the chalkboard. Teachers, in other words, controlled every aspect of the classroom, including how the time was utilized and the furniture was arranged (Cuban, 1984). Unlike student-centered classrooms that function as democratic settings, with shared decision making and concern with learning, teacher-centered classrooms were authoritarian environments, emphasizing unilateral pronouncements and focusing solely on teaching as telling. Since students play important roles in the former, they naturally place a higher value on learning and appear to be more motivated and intellectually engaged.

Change has been slow for several reasons. First, schools have long stressed social control and have functioned as mechanisms for sorting students (Spring, 1976). As Cuban (1984) explains it, recapping this twentieth-century experience:

> [T]he ways schools are organized, the curriculum, and teaching practices mirror the norms of the socio-economic system. Those instructional policies that seek obedience, uniformity, and productivity through, for example, tests, grades, homework, and paying attention to the teacher, prepare children for effective participation in a bureaucratic and corporate culture. Consistent with this argument is that certain teaching practices become functional to achieve these ends: teaching the whole class encourages children to vie for the teacher's attention and encourages competitiveness; teacher questions reward those students who respond with the correct answer; rows of chairs facing a teacher's desk produce a uniform appearance, reinforcing the teacher's authority to control the behavior of the class. . . . Teacher-centered instruction endured because it produces student behaviors expected by the larger society. (p. 9)

Second, school administrators have emphasized efficiency and management, and teachers over time have adapted approaches that achieved these bureaucratic imperatives (Callahan, 1962). "Lecturing, numerous teacher questions, and seatwork are simple ways of conveying knowledge and managing a group efficiently." Third, the teaching culture has maintained a conservative, if not rigid, stance, shunning innovation and preserving tradition. "People who become teachers . . . themselves watched teachers for almost two decades before entering their own classrooms. They tend to use those practices they observed in teachers who taught them" (Cuban, 1984, p. 10). This vicious circle has ensured a stagnant pedagogy, which many students, however, refuse to accept. Fourth, this pedagogical process has functioned as a result of the tacit "treaties" commonly negotiated in high schools, where teachers have demanded little and students have given even less (Powell, Farrar, & Cohen, 1985). This subtle, but profound, disengagement from learning exacerbates student alienation.

Only a few students described their "best" instructors. One female recalled how her favorite teacher taught her about Shakespeare and his works:

I liked *Hamlet*. All the ones like that. I can't remember all of them. We had so many. We had a good English teacher. . . . If kids would have had her, they probably would have liked it. It all depends on who you have. Some people don't give a darn. They say, "Read this." She was like exciting. She was really into it. If you didn't understand it she would help. . . . She would act out a part. Everybody liked her.

Another female informant defined "good" teachers as simply helpful and patient: "They helped you. If you had a problem, they would help you. They would show you as many times as it took. Like math, the teacher would help me with math. He showed me as many times as it took and he wouldn't get mad like most teachers." One African American narrator "loved" her experiences at the "Letsche alternative":

They let you work at your own pace. [Letsche] teachers were not always at the board, doing this and doing that. Coming out, breathing down your neck. I didn't like that. Down in Letsche, if they put some of those teachers in regular high schools, the high schools would be all right.

This student described, in detail, the pedagogical methods of one of her favorite teachers at Letsche:

There was all kinds of tables, you know; there were four of us to a table. She would come to the table. She would help us do our work.

She would laugh with us, and talk with us, you know. The class
was an hour long. We had time to do our work and talk a little bit.
If we needed something, she would always come. We get projects in
the room. Her class was biology. And in biology in [my former high
school], I didn't like it. But when I went to Letsche and did biology,
I made an A.

Therefore, according to the narrators, simple ingredients, like obvious caring or creative pedagogy, defined "good" teachers.

Gender differences may encompass both of these variables. According to Brophy (1985), the classroom routine often reflects the effects of
gender: "Data from several studies suggest that male teachers tend to be
more direct and subject-centered and female teachers to be more indirect
and student-centered" (p. 122). Male instructors prefer to lecture, while
females rely on questioning; males emphasize wrong answers, while
females frequently praise student efforts; and males respond to student failure, while females appear to be warmer and stress success. As a result,
Brophy (1985) asserts:

> Students had more public response opportunities, initiated more private
> contacts with the teachers in classes taught by females. They were also more
> likely to guess when unsure of their answer in female teachers' classes but
> more likely to remain silent in male teachers' classes (suggesting that the
> students felt safer in guessing in the female teachers' classes). (p. 122)

Female instructors, as developmentalists, are more apt to emphasize learning, while males, more often traditionalists, are likely to stress teaching.
Kelly (1993) reinforces Brophy's conclusions, because she observed in her
California interviews that students in traditional, teacher-centered classrooms abandoned learning even though they continued to attend school.

This pattern of differences between male and female teachers, unfore-
seen at first, emerged nevertheless among Pittsburgh's school leavers. Isolated and inferred gender patterns appeared rather than widespread and
blatant ones. Informants voiced complaints about their high school teachers, where male teachers dominate, but never criticized their middle or elementary school instructors. No attempt was made during the interview
process, or subsequent reviews of the typescripts, to quantify narrators'
references to faculty according to gender, yet trends did appear. These students consistently made negative comments about "his class" or "he"; that
is, "poor" teachers generally, but not always, seemed to be males. When
interviewees mentioned "good" instructors, the pronouns "her" and "she"
often appeared.

Students were therefore more positive toward their elementary teachers, who were usually female, than their secondary instructors. A female student expressed deep affection for her elementary teachers: "I loved them all!" She organized a surprise baby shower for her sixth-grade instructor: "Me and my friends got together. She was pregnant. Her birthday was June the sixth. I remember; we all got together, pitched in, and gave her a party. . . . I'm the one who got the party started." Neither this nor any other narrator expressed such ebullience for secondary teachers. A male informant identified his third- and sixth-grade female instructors by name when asked about "good" teachers. "They used to treat me good. They used to be nice to me. They would help me in my work and stuff. . . . Drove me home from school; I used to stay after school and wash the boards." Another male narrator described how one of his elementary instructors sacrificed her personal time for him. "On off days [she] would come to my house, before my mother went blind, and me and her would go on trips, maybe to the mall. She would later take me home and give me a special spelling test or reading test." A fourth student summarized it in this way: Elementary teachers "just cared more and explained. When you get into high school, it is completely different." This difference appeared to center on the teacher's role; that is, elementary teachers comfortably moved beyond the traditional instructor's responsibilities. They clearly cared about the students and expanded their instructional role to compensate for students' needs. These students recognized this nurturing process and appreciated their adult contacts.

Thus, transitions from elementary to middle and high school prove to be more than "ecological stress," that is, not just adjustment to new social and larger physical environments, but include adaptation to educational practices and personal relationships. One informant described her impressions of the differences between elementary and secondary levels: "Middle school and high school is completely different. Teachers teach you. It's the teacher." Roderick (1993) found in her Fall River, Massachusetts, study that

> junior high school teachers were more likely to rely on educational techniques—including public evaluation of students' work, the use of whole class rather than small group instruction, and more rigorous grading procedures—which highlighted and encouraged comparisons of students' abilities, rather than emphasizing individual task mastery and progress. Teachers in junior high school math classrooms placed greater emphasis on discipline and less emphasis on student participation. In addition, students perceived junior high school teachers as less supportive than their elementary school instructors. (p. 134)

These teacher-centered practices intensified at the high school level. The results proved tragic:

> As at-risk students move into middle school and high school, their interactions with school personnel become more anonymous and less supportive, their in-class experiences become less engaging and rewarding, and they receive direct messages in terms of track placement regarding their relative position in their school. (p. 135)

All of this results in student "isolation from that school community" (Roderick, 1993, p. 135; see also Wehlage, Rutter, Smith, Lesko, & Fernandez, 1989). The next step seems to be obvious.

Students responded to uncaring teachers and poor teaching in a number of ways. Some accepted it and continued to attend classes. Others began a gradual disengagement process. Still others simply cut classes. Cutting, or ditching, was a more subtle form of school leaving; that is, these students, while still formally enrolled in school, began to fade out. However, one male student, who resented "dull . . . and very impersonal" instructors, circumvented the entire system by creating his own schedule that was based strictly on the teachers, who "were real helpful. The funny thing about either of these teachers, I wasn't scheduled for their classes. I just got a chance to just come on in. I went to the classes that I thought were informative. . . . They were different than most of my other classes." Students, through their own informal network, knew which teachers were "good" and which were "bad," even before attending their classes, and some adapted accordingly.

WHAT THEY LEARNED

Informants' descriptions of their attitudes about school subject matter focused solely on teachers and teaching skills. Farrell (1990) corroborates this finding with his study of New York City school leavers: "Students distinguish 'good' from 'boring' classes on the basis of the process rather than the content of teaching" (p. 108). A Pittsburgh female student liked her biology course because of its tactile emphasis: "Because you got into it. It wasn't something that they sat up there and taught. They actually let you cut up frogs and things like that." These narrators did not complain about the inherent difficulty of a subject area. Subject mastery and preference rested solely on the teacher and teaching. Another female narrator describing another biology class and instructor liked this subject and pointed directly to the teacher's approach to pedagogy and caring: "What we did. His projects. It was hard, but he made everything look easy. He would explain it real carefully. He would sit down and talk to you. If you didn't know it, he would sit down and talk to you. If he had to show you, he would show you. He would talk to you first. We watched movies and dissected." An African American female student liked her math class also because of the instructor: "I just found math easier than other subjects. I had a nice teacher. She took time. You could come before or after school. She would stay when it was convenient for you. She would always be there." Science and mathematics are usually the bane of many marginal students. Yet, many of these school leavers, in a seemingly atypical fashion, liked them. Good pedagogy and caring made the difference, as we see in this description by a female narrator who intensely disliked her high school history class and contrasted the dreary teaching methods in that class with her middle school experiences:

> They were talking about dead people [laughs]. Dead people—I thought we should be talking about what goes on around at that time, because it would have been more interesting. We could all relate to what was going on. I couldn't get into it. The only way I got interested in it was that one year—eighth grade. We used to play history games, boys against girls. But after that we got up to high school. In high school, they would give you the book, ditto sheets, and give the answer questions, and give you a test on it. I mean that's all that they were doing.

Only a few informants described their preferences for certain subjects regardless of the teacher and pedagogy. They exhibited curiosity about subjects they liked. One African American male liked English because it involved reading. An African American female preferred English and history because she liked to read and learn about the past. She also made positive comments about algebra and Spanish. She enjoyed social studies too, especially a focus on law, since she wanted to become an attorney. She spent so much time completing her homework, often toiling until 2 a.m., that she never participated in extracurricular activities. She abandoned her schooling at age 16 in order to earn a GED and start college a year sooner, at age 17. Leaving school, in this case, represented a "shortcut" to higher education. Finally, many students fondly recalled taking field trips to Pittsburgh's Buhl Planetarium, Heinz Hall for the Performing Arts, and Carnegie Museum and Science Center, and to the Hershey chocolate factory in the eastern part of the state. Most expressed enthusiasm for these learning experiences, which broke the monotony of the classroom routine.

The repetition of subject matter content also bored many students, as reflected by this narrator's comments:

I don't think you should need all of those years in school, because what they was teaching me in tenth grade I had already picked up from the eighth grade. They want you in school 12 years, 13 if you go to kindergarten. I don't think you need all them years of school.

This student had never repeated a grade, yet the subject matter seemed to her to be the same year after year. Still another informant abandoned high school because she felt intellectually unchallenged: "They was giving me the fifth-grade work." The schooling process proved to be valueless to her: "I didn't like it. It wasn't doing nothing for me. I was just going over the same stuff I already knew." In both cases, these narrators felt as though they had been retained, and they remained unchallenged.

Interviews also refuted traditional notions about academic skills and uncovered a different phenomenon, stressing the affective rather than the cognitive realm. Unlike the stereotype, 65 of these young people expressed, in their own ways and words, a consistent interest in, even a love of, reading. This observation was based solely on their formal versus informal reading activities. For example, an African American female informant, early in the interview, claimed that she never seemed to be a good reader in school; however, later in the same interview, in response to a question about casual reading, she claimed to read newspapers and "spooky" books. Others read local newspapers, like the now defunct *Pittsburgh Press*, "to see what is going on," as one student expressed it, or the renowned African American *Pittsburgh Courier*, "'cause it was about Blacks," as another narrator noted. They "browsed" through the usual adolescent magazines, like *Sports Illustrated* and *Seventeen*, or adult ones, such as *Ebony* and *Jet*, or atypical ones, like *Popular Mechanics*. More important, many consumed books—albeit largely escapist ones, like Stephen King's novels, as well as solid literature, by authors like Judy Blume and Edgar Allan Poe. They read for fun. A White female belonged to a Book-of-the-Month club. Another informant recounted her reading experiences as follows: "My mother used to get books. One of the first books was *Catcher in the Rye*. My mother introduced me to *Mommy Dearest*, so I read that." An African American student recalled a similar pattern: "I read books . . . [about] Mandela, Martin Luther King, Jr. . . . biographies. . . . My mother buys them at the store for herself, and I read them." Still another read *Malcolm X*. Finally, one African American female dropback boasted: "I like books. I love novels . . . detective stories, romance, mysteries, things like that. I like Jackie Collins. I like different kinds of books. I even read educational books, too." An

African American male informant loved reading so much that he consumed his mother's nursing aid books, his sister's "college books," as well as his Bible. At least two of our narrators read to their own children. One, who liked to read Shakespeare, read Langston Hughes to her young child.

Few students expressed such enthusiasm for their school textbooks, though, regardless of the subject matter. Teachers and other educators they encountered too often overlooked students' outside entertainment and intellectual interests. These school leavers never recalled encountering an English course that assigned popular novels, or a history class that relied on relevant biographies.

School texts have long been criticized as sterile, dull, and biased (Anyon, 1979, 1983). The Commission on Reading (1984) analyzed the mechanics of reading in American schools, focusing on basal readers. First, textbooks appear to be replete with "bad writing." Regardless of the discipline,

> scholars who have examined subject matter textbooks often have failed to dis-
> cover a logical structure. Sections of many textbooks consist of little more than
> lists of facts loosely related to a theme. Abrupt, unmotivated transitions are
> frequent. Textbooks are as likely to emphasize a trivial detail or a colorful
> anecdote as a fundamental principle. (Commission on Reading, 1984, p. 69)

Second, supplementary materials rarely prove to be more stimulating, adversely affecting pedagogy. Students spend an inordinate amount of time on ancillary resources like "workbooks and skill sheets." Elementary children alone complete 1,000 worksheets a year (Commission on Reading, 1984). These do not require writing or high levels of thinking, and generally appear to be unstimulating. Close adherence to a textbook approach constrains teachers' responses to "learner variation" and inhibits the use of creative approaches (Rozycki, 1992, p. 161). Students, as a result of years of lack of motivation, become bored with their formal reading materials.

Michael Apple (1986) adds a political dimension; that is, texts standardize knowledge that is a part of a "larger system of control" (p. 82). "It is estimated," he continues, "that 75 percent of the time elementary and secondary students are in classrooms and 90 percent of their time on homework is spent with text materials" (p. 85). These required readings define "what is elite and legitimate culture" (p. 81). For Apple (1986),

> the choice of particular content and ways of approaching it in schools is
> related both to existing relations of domination and to struggles to alter these
> relations. Not to recognize this is to ignore a wealth of evidence in the United
> States, England, Australia, France, Sweden, Germany, and elsewhere that
> linked school knowledge—both commodified and lived—to class, gender, and
> race dynamics outside as well as inside an institution of education. (pp. 84–85)

Sterilized textbook knowledge, therefore, anesthetizes students concerning inequality and vital social issues (Claybaugh, 1992). Given this social and political context, it is no surprise that many narrators did indeed read, and preferred biographies about minority struggles and heroes, newspapers, and literature that focused on minorities and minority perspectives. Lack of reading skills did not appear to be a serious problem for these interviewees, but failure to enjoy what was read, that is, the assigned textbooks, contributed to their alienation from reading and ultimately from their school courses.

CONCLUSION

Spradley (1979), operating within a symbolic interactionist framework, defines culture as "the acquired knowledge that people use to interpret experience and generate social behavior" (p. 5). Schools, on the surface, appear to be monolithic, but, upon deeper analysis, host a myriad of cultures. He adds, "Our schools have their own cultural systems and even within the same institution people see things differently" (p. 12). Each group creates its cultural meanings and symbols. Within this dynamic setting, this chapter has isolated school leavers' perceptions of teachers, teaching, and subject matter, and shed light on their culture by using an ethnographic approach, relying on interviews of the participants.

Students entered a large and intimidating high school facility and encountered impersonal, if not hostile, instructors. A social and intellectual gulf existed between teachers and students, and this contributed to school leaving. Teachers in this study may have perceived themselves as competent professionals, being experts in their content fields and ably managing their classrooms, even congratulating themselves on a job well done. However, school leavers saw them differently. They witnessed calloused adults who exhibited little caring toward students and devoted even less energy to creating an exciting learning environment. Success or failure, as these school leavers saw it, was based strictly on their relationships with teachers, and this gives the process of learning a high level of subjective meaning. According to these school leavers, teachers contributed to the school leaver problem. In summary, not one informant described an adult advocate, that is, an administrator or a teacher, who defended the student's interests and needs in school (Wehlage et al., 1989). More than alienation from academic subject matter and other educational and social activities in their schools, students felt estranged from the adults who were supposed to help them.

Educators and policy makers fail to realize the profound impact teachers have on students. Teachers themselves do not understand the important role they play in students' social and intellectual lives. Teachers certainly face significant challenges—few resources, little administrative support, apathetic parents, a hostile public, critical politicians, and unmotivated students. In spite of these overwhelming conditions, teachers maintain the most contact with students, shaping their concepts of school success or failure. Teachers, therefore, possess the power to alter student perceptions of themselves as learners and their relationship to schooling, possibly mitigating school leaving. As one narrator summarized it: "If I could be a teacher for one day, my students would love me. They would love me."

NOTES

This is part of a larger study, Altenbaugh, Engel, and Martin (1995), which reconstructs the entire schooling experience through school leavers' eyes. I am synthesizing the material from that study, especially material that focuses on school leavers' perceptions of teachers. I thank Falmer Press, which holds the copyright, for granting me permission to reproduce portions of that book in this chapter. I also want to thank my coauthors for allowing me to extract material for this chapter.

See Altenbaugh, Engel, and Martin (1995) for a more detailed narrative of the methodological approach used in this study, which conformed to the Human Subjects Guidelines required by the University of Pittsburgh. The original interview process also received clearance from the Department of Labor through the Pittsburgh Job Corps Center. I am grateful for the cooperation and geniality of the Pittsburgh Job Corps staff.

1. See *Pittsburgh Public Schools 1992–93 Dropout Report* (Division of Student Information Management, December 1993), and *Pittsburgh Public Schools, School Profiles: School Year 1992–1993* (Division of Student Information Management, January 1994). The information on class size is found in *Pittsburgh Public Schools Secondary Schools Annual Load Summary Report, 1993–1994 School Year* (Division of Student Information Management, May 1994).

2. All of these data have been culled from *Pittsburgh Public Schools 1992–93 Lunch Application Analysis Report* (Division of Student Information Management, April 5, 1993).

REFERENCES

Altenbaugh, R. J., Engel, D. E., & Martin, D. T. (1995). *Caring for kids: A critical study of urban school leavers*. London: Falmer Press.

Anyon, J. (1979). Ideology and United States history textbooks. *Harvard Educational Review, 49*, 361–386.

Anyon, J. (1983). Workers, labor and economic history, and textbook content. In

M. W. Apple & L. Weis (Eds.), *Ideology and practice in schooling* (pp. 37–60). Philadelphia: Temple University Press.

Apple, M. W. (1986). *Teachers and texts: A political economy of class and gender relations in education.* New York: Routledge.

Beck, L., & Muia, J. A. (1980). A portrait of a tragedy: Research findings on the dropout. *High School Journal, 64,* 65–72.

Bennett, K. P., & LeCompte, M. D. (1990). *The way schools work: A sociological analysis of education.* New York: Longman.

Brophy, J. (1985). Interactions of male and female students with male and female teachers. In L. C. Wilkinson & C. B. Marrett (Eds.), *Influences in classroom interaction* (pp. 115–142). Orlando, FL: Academic Press.

Callahan, R. E. (1962). *Education and the cult of efficiency: A study of the social forces that have shaped the administration of the public schools.* Chicago: University of Chicago Press.

Claybaugh, G. K. (1992). Textbooks and true believers. *Educational Horizons, 70,* 159–161.

Commission on Reading. (1984). *Becoming a nation of readers.* Washington, DC: National Institute of Education.

Cuban, L. (1984). *How teachers taught: Constancy and change in American classrooms, 1890–1980.* New York: Longman.

Farrell, E. (1990). *Hanging in and dropping out: Voices of at-risk high school students.* New York: Teachers College Press.

Kelly, D. M. (1993). *Last chance high: How girls and boys drop in and out of alternative schools.* New Haven: Yale University Press.

Powell, A. G., Farrar, E., & Cohen, D. K. (1985). *The shopping mall high school: Winners and losers in the educational marketplace.* Boston: Houghton Mifflin.

Roderick, M. (1993). *The path to dropping out: Evidence for intervention.* Westport, CT: Auburn Press.

Rozycki, E. G. (1992). The textbook: Tool or symbol? *Educational Horizons, 70,* 161–163.

Rumberger, R. W. (1991). Chicano dropouts: A review of research and policy issues. In R. R. Valencia (Ed.), *Chicano school failure and success: Research and policy agendas for the 1990s* (pp. 64–90). London: Falmer Press.

Spradley, J. P. (1979). *The ethnographic interview.* New York: Holt, Rinehart and Winston.

Spring, J. (1976). *The sorting machine: National educational policy since 1945.* New York: David MacKay.

Stoughton, C. R., & Grady, R. R. (1978). How many students will drop out and why? *North Central Association Quarterly, 53,* 312–315.

Wehlage, G. G., Rutter, R. A., Smith, G. A., Lesko, N., & Fernandez, R. R. (1989). *Reducing the risk: Schools as communities of support.* London: Falmer Press.

CHAPTER 4

The Professionally Challenged Teacher: Teachers Talk About School Failure

ELEANOR BLAIR HILTY

Public schools have occupied an important place in the growth and progress of the United States. The aims and purposes of these schools often have shifted as they have been asked to address and even ameliorate a wide range of social ills. Public schools seemed to capture the spirit and dreams of a new country seeking to merge the lives and identities of many people into something uniquely American. These early schools can even be considered innovative, in the sense that they were envisioned by our predecessors as a democratic solution to the education issue. Private schools for the elite would continue to exist, but public schools provided a vehicle for the masses to acquire formal schooling and benefit from the "uplifting" effect of a general education. Greene (1985) argues, "Surely it is an obligation of education in a democracy to empower the young to become members of the public, to participate, and play articulate roles in the public space" (p. 4). Public schools in America became the cornerstone for this philosophical orientation; the place where equality of opportunity translated to equality of *educational* opportunity. To many people it seemed essential that we provide a free, public education that would be common to *all* children and teach common values, beliefs, and attitudes necessary for participation in the democratic process and responsible citizenry. In a relatively short period of time, *common* schools became the norm in this country, and they rapidly were accompanied by the emergence of compulsory school laws encouraging law-abiding parents to entrust the public schools with the primary responsibility for educating their children. Thus, over the past 150 years, an increasing number of school-age children have attended public schools that attempt to provide for all children the prerequisite knowledge and skills for survival: cognitively, socially, politically, and economically. Despite popular beliefs to the contrary, most Americans continue to endorse the concept of a publicly supported public school, and consistently demonstrate this by sending their children to the public schools located in their communities. And, generally speaking, public schools are successful experiences for many children. However, the children for whom the public schools are not successful experiences are increasingly the source of concern, and the subject of considerable debate, in discussions of school reform.

Perhaps it is not surprising that we have placed upon this institution tremendous expectations for the exercise of democratic principles and the provision of equality of educational opportunity. Beane and Apple (1995) consider the relationship of these democratic ideals to discussions of school reform:

> Many of our most trusted and powerful ideas about schooling are the hard-won gains of long and courageous efforts to make our schools more democratic. We are the beneficiaries of those efforts, and we have an obligation to carry forward the demanding dream of public schools for a democratic society. . . . Although our memories may have become blurred, we can still recall that public schools are essential to democracy. We cannot help but be jolted wide awake when discussions about what works in schools, what should be done in schools, make no mention of the role of public schools in expanding the democratic way of life. (p. 4)

Unfortunately, the public schools are forced to regularly address the contradictions inherent in discussions of "equality of educational opportunity." Does "equality of educational opportunity" mean an "equal chance" or an "equal share"? The competing tensions between the pursuit of equity *and* that of excellence in public schools have characterized most discussions of failure and, consequently, most recommendations for reform. Is it possible to do both—provide equitable educational experiences *and* promote excellence in the schools? For example, the much-publicized *America 2000* was a strategy initiated by President Bush in 1991 for achieving six National Education Goals for reforming and restructuring American education through an emphasis on excellence in our public schools. This effort was supported by the governors of all 50 states and thus recognizes the overall importance of the role played by public schools. However, the reconciliation of attempts to provide equitable educational experiences *and* promote excellence is difficult at best. *America 2000* and the National Education Goals, subsequently revised to include two additional goals, provide support for increased rigor and higher standards for public schools. Yet this national agenda ignores the reality that characterizes the lives of an increasingly large number of children who live in poverty.

If school achievement and success are essential to one's survival in this society, what does one do with the specter of school failure in our discussions of equity *and* excellence in the public schools? How does one answer the most frequently asked question in these discussions: "Who do we blame for this problem?" Is this a social problem or an educational problem? How can it be that in a country devoted to the ideals of equal educational opportunity, so many children who come from less advantaged backgrounds fail to succeed? Erickson (1984) attempts to answer this question as follows:

> Given that for approximately 5 million years human societies have managed to rear their young so that almost every one in the society was able to master the knowledge and skills necessary for survival, why does this not happen in modern societies with schools? Or does it happen—do schools teach what is necessary, but define and measure achievement in such ways that it looks as if large proportions of the school population fail? (p. 527)

Have public schools simply lost touch with the "knowledge and skills necessary for survival"? The education provided by many schools may lack relevance to the lives of children who come from diverse sociocultural backgrounds. In most contemporary school environments, the strict regulation of curriculum requirements and the use of standardized measures of achievement often shift the focus from "teaching the child" to "teaching the test." In this way, students are denied access to "culturally relevant teaching" and, consequently, to the knowledge and skills necessary for survival in a variety of contexts. Ladson-Billings (1994) expands this idea:

> Culturally relevant teaching uses student culture in order to maintain it and to transcend the negative effects of the dominant culture. The negative effects are brought about, for example, by not seeing one's history, culture, or background represented in the textbook or curriculum or by seeing that history, culture, or background distorted. . . . Specifically, culturally relevant teaching is a pedagogy that empowers students intellectually, socially, emotionally, and politically by using cultural referents to impart knowledge, skills, and attitudes. These cultural referents are not merely vehicles for bridging or explaining the dominant culture; they are aspects of the curriculum in their own right. (pp. 17–18)

The knowledge and skills proffered in many classrooms may be prerequisite to higher levels of academic achievement in traditionally organized educational institutions, but have little value in urban, inner-city neigh-borhoods or even isolated, rural communities where "survival" means very different things to very different populations of children. The skills and knowledge necessary to survive in urban ghettos or small, rural commu-nities may be counterproductive or even mutually exclusive to the acqui-sition of "mainstream" values, beliefs, and attitudes.

SCHOOL FAILURE

The American dream has always been that all children, regardless of per-sonal circumstances, have a chance, in this country, to become anyone or anything they desire. For many children these dreams originated in class-rooms and schools where hard work was rewarded by academic successes. Most important, academic success in the public schools opened up the doors of higher education and provided unlimited opportunities for high-status jobs and social mobility. This was "the dream": hard work + good schools = success! Of course, "success" as it is broadly defined can mean many things to many people, but at its simplest level, it means "choice"—a conscious choice to make dreams a reality. The reality, however, is not so simple. Schools fail, and most important, children fail. In these situations, hard work is not rewarded with success, instead the efforts of both teachers and stu-dents produce little visible evidence of those things most valued by critics of the public schools, for example, high test scores and verbally precocious, well-mannered children. The "failures" of these schools, such as dropouts or students with low levels of academic performance, offend those individu-als who still believe that the American dream is alive and well. However, the truth about the "dream" is that some children consistently fail more than others, and that poor children of color in this country experience school fail-ure at a considerably higher rate than other children. And yet, as increasing numbers of children "fail" to demonstrate the requisite skills and knowledge that would characterize a school as "successful," it would seem imperative that critical educators begin to examine this phenomenon from a broader perspective. This is a perspective that recognizes how "school failure is struc-turally located and culturally mediated" (McLaren, 1994, p. 216). In effect, it is a recognition of the roles played by both institutional and cultural vari-ables that will shift the focus from solutions that isolate individual "prob-lems" to the acknowledgment of community "problems" that begin outside of schools, but ultimately affect the "success" or "failure" of all students.

Ladson-Billings (1994) points out in this regard that "an often-asked question of people of color, women, and other marginalized groups is, 'What is it you people want?' Surprisingly for some, what these people want is not very different from what most Americans want: an opportunity to shape and share in the American dream" (p. 137). Consider the following:

> The American commitment to equality of opportunity is violated at its very roots by the fact that local and state governments continue to pay more for one child's education than for another's. The abiding constants of American education—equality of opportunity and meritocracy—favor existing elites and place minority students in the debt column of the ledger of academic achievement. . . . Of course, poverty is a major factor in determining the success of students at school. It is perhaps the greatest predictor of academic success in this country, which makes it disturbing to learn that in 1988, only 25 percent of three- and four-year-olds with family incomes of less than $10,000 a year were enrolled in a preschool program. Yet 56 percent of those with family incomes of $35,000 or more were enrolled. More than one-third of all children in families headed by someone younger than thirty are living in poverty. (McLaren, 1994, pp. 15–16, 23)

The tragedy is that those children who most need successful school experiences for safe passage to adulthood are those for whom these experiences are most often characterized as "failures." These children often see their future choices narrowed rather than expanded due to their school experiences.

Some of the most disturbing questions concerning school failure focus on "the strong relationship between family background and educational achievement" (Dougherty & Hammack, 1990, p. 2). Why should poor children consistently fail to achieve in schools at rates comparable to their more affluent peers? Recent projections show a growing Hispanic population, with half of these children living in poverty by 2010. Add to these figures documentation that these children often do poorly in school and drop out of school at an earlier age and a higher rate than Black or White students ("Half of Black, Hispanic Children May Be Poor by 2010," 1993). "Students who were Black or Hispanic, living in families with low income, or living in the South or West were less likely to complete high school," and the dropout rate for Hispanic students is nearly triple the national figure ("High Percentage of Female High School Dropouts Quit," 1994, p. 6A). Questions about school failure and the integrity of the school experience often are linked together, and the implications are alarming. If the public schools are to continue to function as they have in the past, then their roles and responsibilities must be redefined in such a way as to justify the consumption of vast resources under the guise of providing a free and equitable public education for the masses. Dramatic changes are, almost certainly, necessary. Yet, issues related to school failure, while complex and multidimensional, are constantly in flux. Meaningful changes in the schools must simultaneously address the needs of schools today as well as schools for the twenty-first century. What will not change, however, is the central importance of a successful educational experience, and for a majority of children that experience probably will occur in the public schools; there may be no other alternatives.

Explanations for school failure usually cannot be traced to a single variable. Rather, every aspect of the educational experience is subject to scrutiny. Familial, societal, and institutional forces frequently are interconnected, and all contribute to the net outcome of school failure. Blame often shifts back and forth between the school and the family environment. Researchers traditionally have focused on "pupils' deficiencies (lack of ability or motivation, often due to a poor home life) or teachers' deficiencies (lack of ability, poor training, or inadequate standards)" (Dougherty & Hammack, 1990, p. 3). Thus, research efforts in this area have been concerned with disputing or augmenting these "traditional" explanations. What are the intersections between the traditional explanations and those explanations that emphasize the often neglected voices of teachers and students and recognize the power of individual action? Far less information is available about the "worlds" of those teachers and students who are expected to spend 180 days a year in schools characterized by a high level of failure. It would seem apparent to the casual observer that this type of schooling experience is qualitatively different from the experiences of those teachers and students who inhabit the worlds of fairly affluent suburban schools where the focus is on school success, both individual and group. How does failure mediate the teaching and learning experiences of the inhabitants of these "other worlds"?

TEACHERS AND FAILURE

Most of the time the students are the *only* source of rewards for most teachers. Isolated in their own classrooms, teachers receive feedback for their efforts from the words, expressions, behaviors, and suggestions of the students. By doing well on a test, sharing a confidence, performing a task, indicating an interest, and reporting the effects of a teacher's influence, students let teachers know that they are doing a good job and are appreciated. Unlike other professionals who look to colleagues and supervisors for such feedback, teachers can only turn to children. (Lieberman & Miller, 1990, p. 194)

Failure. Nothing else diminishes the worth and value of a teacher's work more than the pervading sense of failure that surrounds the schools attended by poor children and children of color in America. Their problems are both demographic as well as geographic. Schools in states that consistently score low on all measures of school success are perceived as inadequate and their students as inferior. These schools often suffer from a lack of resources, both economic and political. This lack of resources often leads to pejorative characterizations of the children as "at risk." What are the implications of calling poor children or children of color "at risk"? Are they really at risk only of failing to become middle class? William Ayers (1994) questions: "Is calling someone culturally deprived the same as calling them not white, not middle class? . . . Is the implication that some cultures are superior and others inferior?" (p. 10). And then what about the teachers? Teachers, both urban and rural, who work in schools characterized by high levels of failure (high dropout rates, low achievement, low levels of literacy, etc.) are a special population. Is it not possible that these teachers also can be considered an "at-risk" population? Might this be a useful categorization for teachers who are professionally challenged by the day-to-day failures they encounter in the classroom? We want to believe that good teachers don't fail, and yet we all know that is not true. It will never be satisfactory to measure the goodness and worth of a teacher's performance strictly by looking at student outcomes. And yet, close proximity to failure carries with it a stigma. Failure is insidious to the committed professional; it feels bad personally and professionally. Public attacks on the "failures" of our schools often accompany demands for teacher accountability. Implicit in the demands for "teacher accountability" is the belief that good teachers don't fail. Viewed in this context, student failure equals teacher failure; thus, nothing affronts the professional identities of teachers more than school failure, and all of the negative connotations that accompany these losses. Finally, to an already skeptical public, school failure is just one more reminder of the terrible inadequacies of the public schools.

My work with teachers, as a teacher educator and researcher, often has brought me face-to-face with teachers who, while basically satisfied with their roles as teachers, have complex professional lives that do not lend themselves easily to celebratory accounts of the joys of teaching. The lives of these teachers are fraught with frustrations, and the job most often is not at all what they were anticipating when they began teaching. Many of these teachers leave within the first 5 years of teaching. Interviews I conducted in the late 1980s (summarized in Hilty, 1987) provided the following first-person accounts of what it is like to be a teacher:

> Teaching is not what I expected. When I grew up in rural West
> Virginia and went to school, I remember what teachers did and I
> remember the role that they played. There was pride in teaching.
> High school teachers were looked at as leaders in the community

and people that you looked up to. Those days are gone. People feel, and I didn't realize this until I was teaching, it's kinda degrading to say, "I'm a high school teacher." You have to say it under your breath. I used to think people had a lot of respect for high school teachers, but I feel that they don't anymore. It's just a guy who wants to teach school is just the attitude I get now. That's kind of an embarrassment to me because I do enjoy it. (Vocational-Technical Preparation Teacher)

You're expected to do so much and you feel, it's just like well, can't you individualize for these seventeen people here, and there's no way you can individualize all day long. You're going to have to have a group, and some of them are going to get it and some of them aren't going to get it. You know, I get really frustrated with the numbers that we have. Seems like every time I turn around, there's somebody else coming in, but no more help. You get real frustrated. Most teachers, I think, would do away with money, if they could have fewer children in their room. (Middle Grades Teacher)

I would just love to work with new special education teachers and help them avoid the kinds of pitfalls that lead to nothing but frustration and feelings of doubt and lack of self-worth and all the things that go with being special education. The retarded teacher does become the *retarded* teacher rather than the teacher of children who are limited. (Special Education Teacher)

I would say the main thing that depressed me was the kids' low motivations. They didn't want to be there at all. (Middle Grades Teacher)

It seems important that we concern ourselves with the "nature" of the experience of those teachers who do stay. How do they perceive their jobs and, most important, what is the relationship between teacher success and student success? Obviously, some teachers perceive and define their jobs in such a way that student success, as it traditionally has been defined, is not vital to their understanding of professional identity and integrity. Foster (1993) suggests:

Although there is a large body of literature on teacher thinking, planning, and practical knowledge, it does not focus specifically on successful teachers who work with students who are currently defined and pejoratively labeled as "at risk." As a result, we know little about the thinking, pedagogical processes, understandings, or considerations, of such teachers, nor do we understand how many of these teachers define their teaching situation, decide which roles and responsibilities to assume, and apply this knowledge to their practice. . . . How is it that successful teachers of "at-risk" children define their tasks and what is their understanding of the goals of successful teaching? (pp. 390–391)

Any exploration or discussion of teachers' lives ultimately must consider the relationship between student success (or lack thereof) and teachers' perceptions of their roles and responsibilities.

Is student success a reliable measure of a teacher's effectiveness or commitment? Of course not, but increasingly this view is being challenged by a focus on teacher accountability that quickly becomes narrowly defined as measurable success (i.e., increased student achievement on standardized tests). Since the late 1980s, there has been an explosion of research that provides first-person accounts of teachers' experiences in the classroom. This literature is replete with discussions of the many "failures" of our society generally and of the schools specifically. Teachers who regularly live their professional lives in environments characterized by a high level of failure have been explored only within the context of *a* successful classroom or *a* successful teacher. Whenever I read these descriptions I applaud the successful innovations of individual teachers in selected classrooms, but I also wonder, What about the rest of *them*? What are *they* doing? Were *they* equally successful? Erickson (1984) recounted the story of a young Eskimo who learned to hunt seal from his father. The young man was advised that "if you want to hunt seal you have to learn to think like a seal" (p. 527). Likewise, if one wants to understand, identify, or even train good teachers who are successful with at-risk students, one has to understand the cognitive strategies of those teachers who are successful with these students. In this chapter, I have tried to provide a forum for *those* teachers—a place where their voices can be heard; a place where others can attempt to better understand the factors that help teachers reconcile their professional identities with the phenomenon of school failure. Additionally, I have tried to consider the implications of this knowledge for all teachers, preservice and inservice.

CONTEXTUALIZING SCHOOL FAILURE

In 1987, I moved to Atlanta, Georgia, to teach at a local college. During the next 6 years, I had the opportunity to work with teachers from both urban and rural schools in the South. As an educational foundations professor, I was often responsible for providing a broader context for their discussions of teaching and learning as well as success and failure in schools besieged by the contemporary problems of American youth. The experience was unsettling. As I listened to these teachers, I began to notice some real differences in the ways that they perceived their experiences. Two groups of teachers seemed to emerge: those who were challenged, and even enjoyed, teaching in schools characterized by a high level of failure, and those who perceived these experiences as discouraging and hopeless. What was the difference? Was it something so simple as attitude or something more personal having to do with the "meaning" they attach to a teacher's roles and responsibilities and student success and failure? Schubert (1991) encourages researchers to recognize "*teacher lore* as a necessary and neglected construct in educational literature" (p. 207), and discusses the relevance of this kind of knowledge:

> I characterize teacher lore as the study of the knowledge, ideas, perspectives, and understandings of teachers. In part, it is inquiry into the beliefs, values, and images that guide teachers' work. In this sense, it constitutes an attempt to learn what teachers learn from their experience. Teachers are continuously in the midst of a blend of theory (their evolving ideas and personal belief systems) and practice (their reflective action); I refer to this blend as *praxis*. To assume that scholarship can focus productively on what teachers learn recognizes teachers as important partners in the creation of knowledge about education. (p. 207)

Thus, viewed in this manner, an understanding of how teachers "succeed" in environments characterized by high levels of school failure becomes an important source of information.

Initially, it was my hypothesis that these two groups of teachers were fundamentally different, but the nature of these differences was unclear. Some teachers obviously define their work in such a way that student success and teacher success are interpreted in a broader context, and that student success as we traditionally define it may not be a factor in the experience of "successful" teaching. Is it possible that these teachers succeed, where others fail, because of these differences in perception? Erickson (1986) argues that we should explore the "conditions of meaning" or "meaning systems" that enable some students to learn and others not. Perhaps we should conduct the same explorations with teachers. What "meanings" allow some teachers to succeed where others have found only failure and burnout. Psychologists tell us that past experiences and expectations mediate perceptions, and thus one might examine the worlds of successful teachers in order to better understand the manner in which they structure their experiences. It would seem that a better understanding of *who* these teachers are and *how* they define their tasks and endeavors to be "successful" teachers in environments that provide very few indicators of success (e.g., student achievement, high test scores, positive feedback, professional recognition, etc.), would be timely and appropriate. In collaboration and dialogue with these teachers, we learn that "teachers inquire deeply and their lives and stories cannot be revealed without a sense of the 'research' they live but rarely write about" (Schubert, 1991, p. 224).

Ogbu (1990) warns social scientists that "in their eagerness to bring about change, they often design their studies not so much to understand the total situation as to discover *what is wrong* and how the situation should be changed." His final caution is worthy of consideration: "This approach leads to the wrong kinds of questions, the wrong kinds of answers and the wrong kinds of solutions" (p. 398). He is telling us that the questions we ask often determine the answers. If we talk about student failure as a family or environmental problem or even as a societal problem, we predefine and set the parameters of the research we are doing. Heeding this warning, I set out to design a study that would help me better understand and describe the phenomenon of school failure from the teacher's perspective. During the past 2 years I have discussed school failure with five teachers. I used life and career interviews to inquire about the teachers' personal and professional backgrounds. I conducted and recorded these interviews in the teachers' homes. Each interview lasted from 1 to 2 hours. These teachers represented a diverse group, with the common denominator being that each one elected to teach in a school characterized by a high level of student failure as it traditionally is defined. All of the schools discussed by these teachers serve students who come from less advantaged backgrounds. Children of color represented a significant portion of the student body at these schools. Two of the teachers were Black and three were White. All of these teachers would characterize themselves as middle class; however, their backgrounds reflect a broad range of both cultural and economic experiences. The range of teaching experience among these teachers ranged from 6 to 20 years. In these interviews, I posed very general and open-ended questions and tried to give teachers an opportunity to construct their own "pictures" of classroom life. After they initially told me about themselves and their educational backgrounds, I asked the following kinds of questions:

1. Tell me about teaching.
2. Tell me about the children you teach.
3. Tell me about those children who succeed in your class.
4. Tell me about those children who fail in your class.
5. Tell me how you feel when students succeed.
6. Tell me how you feel when students fail.

7. What are the satisfactions/dissatisfactions of teaching?
8. Given a choice, would you keep teaching? Would you request a transfer? Why or why not?

According to Kvale (1983), the purpose of such an interview "is to gather descriptions of the life-world of the interviewee with respect to interpretation of the meaning of the described phenomena" (p. 174). The use of this kind of interview is intended to provide a place where "ordinary people are able to describe their own life-world, their opinions and acts, in their own words. . . . The interview makes it possible for the subjects to organize their own descriptions, emphasizing what they themselves find important" (p. 173). In these interviews, the experience of student failure and success is described from the teacher's perspective.

THE TEACHERS TALK

All of these teachers described the children they teach as at-risk populations from less advantaged backgrounds. It is with some level of discomfort that I use the term *at risk* to describe students who experience a lack of success in the public schools. Educators have employed various terminology to describe the concept of at-risk students for over 200 years (Cuban, 1989; Swadener, 1990). It usually refers to students possessing various traits that put them at risk for dropping out of school. Swadener argues that there is ample evidence that social class is a major risk factor for many students. However, in addition to being at risk for dropping out of school, these teachers also discussed other variables that placed their students at risk. Students who fail also were described as being at risk for the following reasons:

- *Low socioeconomic status and socialization patterns that influence the range of choices and options available to them*

Barely surviving . . . very difficult for them to be consistent doing anything. . . . Their parents don't have the skills necessary to make that child successful.

No efforts made to help children realize their choices and the impact of those choices.

- *Low expectations for achievement and ambiguous instructional goals*

What then can they take? Level 1 students. . . . They've already failed the lowest-level classes. . . . We aren't teaching them.

* *Residing in communities that often are isolated and tend to provide few positive role models of academic success*

They don't have anyone to expose them, so to speak, to the finer things in life. . . . If a teacher doesn't do it, then it's not gonna get done because their parents aren't concerned or they just don't think it's important to expose their children to a play, to expose their children to a museum—those sort of things. Now we can expose our children to watching *Boyz in the Hood* on TV or at the theater, but we're not going to expose our children to the museum in downtown Atlanta.

Despite the concerns and connotations surrounding the use of the term *at risk*, it was nonetheless the preferred terminology of the teachers in this study. Caution should always be used in characterizing groups of individuals based on predetermined notions of success that require, as prerequisites, strictly ordained behaviors, values, attitudes, and beliefs. However, in keeping with the original intent of this study, I have remained faithful to the language and meanings used by the teachers.

The Experience of Teaching Children Who Are At Risk

Teachers are affected by student failure . . . it disturbs them . . . frustrates . . . it makes them sad and sometimes makes them angry . . . teachers as frustrated as the students . . . ultimately it causes them to question their integrity as professionals . . . question the curriculum . . . question the values and beliefs of a discipline.

The problems just are so deep-rooted . . . now, whose fault is it . . . I didn't take it as my fault that these kids were in the predicament that they were in . . . but, you can't point the finger at parents, teachers, administrators . . . we're all in this together . . . it's just overwhelming.

I think sometimes, OK, how much is mine . . . how much responsibility [for their failure] . . . constantly make changes . . . different group, different stuff . . . I will try anything to make all of my kids feel a part of my program.

The only way we [the teachers] made it through was by getting together and talking about it daily.

> Other teachers talk about it [failure] . . . administrators talk about it . . . even distribute lists of teachers with accompanying rates of failure . . . teachers with high levels of failure feel defensive.

> There are times that just . . . I think I've had it . . . I can't come back next year . . . I've just had too much, but the rest during the summer always has me ready . . . I am so ready to go back in August.

The experience of teaching at-risk students caused a response that was both physical and emotional. While each of these teachers freely elected to work with at-risk students, the language they used to describe their experiences nonetheless reflected the stress and difficulty inherent to these tasks. Their efforts brought them together and created bonds among teachers and between students. They were often frustrated; however, it seemed that a symbiotic relationship developed. Student success, however small, was perceived as teacher success, and student failure was perceived as teacher failure. Failure was "bad," and there were negative connotations associated with its close proximity to one's classroom. However, for these teachers, the response caused them to "pull together" as a group and rethink their roles and responsibilities, rather than "pull out," both emotionally and intellectually, and finally request a transfer to another school. They felt responsible for the students in their classes. This seemed a healthy response in that these teachers obviously felt a level of control over their professional lives. These teachers accepted the challenge and committed themselves to successful school experiences for students and teachers. They did not focus on issues of blame and responsibility; they were empowered by the experience of empowering the young people for whom they felt responsible.

Teaching and Learning

> How well I perform up here and whether or not they're learning . . . it was like I all of a sudden got over on the other side of the desk in my mind, inside the student . . . Is the student learning? . . . All of a sudden it was like this awakening for me that was what mattered . . . *Is he learning?*

> I know that I don't understand as much as I should about how difficult it is for the children. . . . I try, but I know it's just not there.

> How can you *not* treat them differently because we're not all created out of the same mold . . . I will treat one child differently

from another child if I feel like that's what has to be done in order to get that child involved in what's going on.

Teaching and learning were major concerns for these teachers. Much of their reflection, and subsequent action, was concentrated on creating a "space" for each child to learn. In contrast to many classrooms, these teachers recognized the idiosyncratic nature of the learning difficulties these students were experiencing. The focus was on adapting teaching strategies to facilitate successful learning for *each* child. The task was not perceived as insurmountable, but rather these teachers attempted to visualize and better understand the students' perspective. The students were not seen as unteachable. The task became one of looking at the *individual* and trying to understand her or his perspective on what was happening in the classroom. No one strategy was described by any teacher; rather, teacher attitude or perspective seemed to inform a classroom vision.

Other Teachers, "The Wall," and Learning

Teachers so often have this wall up between them and their [students] . . . particularly White females with a Black student . . . they put up a wall . . . they've got to make it through this the best they can . . . they've got to get their defenses up . . . they're not being open and honest . . . subject-oriented instead of student-oriented . . . I think that they (the other teachers) would go ahead and have class if none showed up.

The content . . . they can't even concentrate on the content until they feel they can work on this and be successful at it . . . my content's important . . . the kid's feeling of self-worth and having confidence comes first.

When you have kids write . . . and they bare their souls in their writing and they feel like they know you on a different level than their math teacher. I don't put a wall in front of me that I am the teacher and you're the kid.

The "wall" metaphor was used frequently by the teachers in this study. It was used to describe the real or imagined barriers that prevent teachers from reaching troubled students. Surmounting those barriers created by race, gender, and social class was the focus of the pedagogical strategies employed by these teachers. They were openly critical of teachers who showed more concern with content than with students. Their visualization of this "connection" between student and teacher established a bond that guided teacher action at a visceral level. "Breaking down the wall" transcended the mere academic goals of most programs and made the needs of students a top priority.

It seems reasonable to consider the relationship between student and teacher as a form of social capital. Wehlage (1993) described this phenomenon as the "shared attitudes, norms and values that promote trust and common expectations" (p. 3). Many of the students discussed by these teachers came from single-parent homes that were perceived as lacking the clear and consistent norms and expectations generally associated with successful school performance. The establishment of a close, caring relationship with a teacher may help to build a strong social connection with a positive role model. This kind of relationship becomes more important than knowledge acquisition in that it provides for these students an important prerequisite to successful learning: a sense of love and belonging. Furthermore, Wehlage (1993) suggests that "in the absence of social capital, children are growing up without strong connections to adults and adult values and institutions. Aimless, norm-less, and increasingly violence-prone youth are the product" (p. 4). Seen in this manner, "breaking down the wall" becomes an important, and often neglected, role of teachers in schools characterized by a high level of failure.

Love?

> "Becoming Real" in the classroom . . . I have to learn to love the kids in front of me . . . I make up my mind that I am going to make him think I love him . . . and usually what happens is that I pretend and play at it . . . he can think it . . . then he starts becoming more lovable and therefore I can love him.

> I love being there . . . being in the classroom . . . being in the school environment. Love them.

> There is hope now. . . . They know when you care about them . . . [I] want to be there.

What has love got to do with it? All teachers love children, right? Well, maybe. These teachers, in particular, insisted on talking about love. The day-to-day challenge of teaching these kids was exciting, but it was love that kept bringing them back year after year. These teachers are passionate about their work and their students. More important, perhaps, is the possibility that this kind of attitude in a teacher leads to strategies that invite students into classroom communities where they encounter respectful, affirming relations that are truly supportive of student success, academically and personally. Kohn (1991) believes that schools should be the sites of this kind of behavior, but too often this is not the case:

> If we had to pick a logical setting in which to guide children toward caring about, empathizing with, and helping other people, it would be a place where they would regularly come into contact with their peers and where some sort of learning is already taking place. The school is such an obvious choice that one wonders how it could be that the active encouragement of prosocial values and behavior—apart from occasional exhortation to be polite—plays no part in the vast majority of American classrooms. (p. 497)

Witherell and Noddings (1991) also share a belief in the importance of caring, concerned, and committed relationships and the dialogue these connections facilitate:

> A caring relation also requires dialogue. The material of dialogue is usually words, but touch, smiles, affectionate sounds and silences, and glances may also be part of it. True dialogue is open; that is, conclusions are not held to be absolute by any party at the outset. The search for enlightenment, responsible choice, perspective, or means to solve a problem is mutual and marked by appropriate signs of reciprocity. (p. 7)

For many students, this bonding with a particular teacher may mark their first, and most significant, positive interaction in a school setting. Farrell (1990) found that among at-risk high school students,

> [t]he school years students identified as their best often involved having a teacher who "cared about me," who "wanted me to learn," who "took a real interest in me." . . . There must be someone in the student's life who values her and who values education and whom the student can remember with admiration and respect. Such a teacher can compensate for the student's lack of academic success. (p. 112)

Thus, while love and a sense of mission seldom are discussed in conjunction with school failure, they seem to play an important role in the lives of teachers who elect to teach children who are "dismissed," figuratively and literally, from our schools. Love initiates a dialogue that lays the foundation for a successful, and reciprocal, teaching and learning experience.

The "Challenge" to Succeed

As a teacher, I want to feel like what I am doing is important, not just that I am teaching them science, but that not only do I teach them science, but they want to learn. . . . The thing that I am looking for is for me to try as hard as I can to grab all of those kids, it's like a challenge—can I grab a kid who runs around on the street and sells drugs, and can I do something that grabs his attention even if it's for 2 days out of 5 in the classroom?—and I've found that almost inevitably I can do that through "hands-on" science and "stand-on-my-head" math, and issuing challenges where they feel successful. . . . I give them 100% before they give it back to me. . . . It is 95% challenge . . . I make a difference in a child a day.

I asked to give up my advanced classes and take basic level kids. . . . I saw us giving those kids to our weakest teachers. . . . I think the other teachers admired the fact that I did it because it was my choice. . . . If I kept saying they needed to have a good teacher, then I decided I would give them one.

There's a challenge everyday . . . there's a challenge to get them interested in what I am teaching. . . . I am never totally satisfied . . . OK, my job is done . . . there's always something else, and once I finish this, there's 12 or 13 other things to choose from that I can work on next . . . or make my goal . . . my next goal . . . I think I would be so dissatisfied if I didn't feel like there was somebody that I needed to work on . . . or some little thing. . . . Teachers have to be willing to do whatever it takes. . . . It is our responsibility to make the kids feel successful.

In a profession frequently characterized by a lack of autonomy, self-esteem, and rewards, it is somewhat surprising that these teachers feel challenged, and even rewarded, by their work with at-risk kids. The challenge of teaching these kids provided a degree of autonomy that allowed them to redefine their roles and responsibilities in the classroom in such a way that succeeding where other teachers had failed led to increased levels of self-confidence and the intrinsic rewards that come from successfully meeting a challenge head-on. Every teacher I talked to in conjunction with this study emphasized the challenge of teaching at-risk students. Data from the U.S. Department of Commerce indicate that the "most common reason for [students] dropping out still is a plain dislike of school" ("High Percentage of Female High School Dropouts Quit," 1994, p. 6A). These teachers repeatedly articulated a desire not only to help students succeed academically, but to improve their overall experience in school. This challenge seemed to appeal to the perceived or real needs of these teachers—the *need* to be needed, the *need* to do something important or even impossible, the *need* to be creative and innovative in the classroom, and even the *need* to make kids feel successful. They wanted to be needed, and these students did, indeed, need good teachers committed to their success. Just as important, however, these teachers wanted to teach low-achieving students who would "push" them to be the best and most innovative teachers they were capable of being. It was a relationship that worked. These were not teachers who desired comfortable jobs; the challenge was everything to these teachers. These teachers understood and recognized the importance of creating close, personal communities in classrooms, "spaces" where student voices were heard and respected. A spirit of cooperative action and interdependence was modeled and lived out within the microcosms of these individual classrooms. This was an important feature of the experience and seemed to be key to the success of both teachers and students.

Black Teachers and Black Students

The aforementioned themes represent clusters and categories of meaning that were present in all of the interviews. However, two of the teachers interviewed were Black, and it is impossible to ignore the most salient differences in the ways that they described their experiences. Both Black teachers had grown up in fairly homogeneous Black communities and attended less advantaged public schools. Both teachers had been successful academically and considered themselves, at this time, to be solidly middle class. They viewed the public schools as very positive influences in their lives. While it is not possible to generalize the experiences of two Black teachers to all Black teachers in the inner city, it was clear that these teachers were frustrated by the high incidence of failure among children of color. The following are representative quotes:

> Done it through hard work on my own. . . . *I* had parental support. I felt like that I was comin' there each day to baby-sit . . . to tell the kids what they're supposed to do . . . not to teach math because in trying to teach them, I didn't. . . . They're not ready.

> It just got to be so many problems where when you hear stuff, you're like . . . I'm sorry, but I am here to teach you math. If you need help, let me refer you to someone else. I really can't hear about it.

Despite the incidence of failure and frustration, these teachers wanted to teach Black children. A unique feature of their frustration was the strong identification and commitment they felt with their students. This attachment was poignantly expressed in the following quotes:

> I felt a need to work with children that were in the Black community . . . I wanted to give back to our community what was given to me . . . seemed like it would be something that would meet my needs as a teacher. . . . We understand the children. You gotta understand the Black culture. . . . They're the same as me. When I look at those kids and I look at me—I see no difference. We're the same.

> I really and truly believe that in order to teach Black inner-city children you need to understand their culture. You need to understand their upbringing . . . be able to relate to it. . . . Our values are being placed on them and they can't relate to them. . . . You're gonna have to almost visualize yourself being in there.

In Foster's (1993) interviews with exemplary African American teachers, a teacher expressed a similar idea:

> Black people have to convince Blacks of how important it [education] is. And how they are all part of that Black umbilical cord because a lot of [Black] teachers, they don't do it consciously, but we are forgetting about our roots, about how we're *connected to this cord*, and about everyone we've left behind. We have it now, and we don't have time for the so-called underclass. But we have to educate ourselves as a group because otherwise what's going to happen to us all? You see what I mean. If I can't see that kid out there in the biggest project, if I can't see how he and I or she and I are of the same *umbilical cord* and do not strive to make us more *connected to that cord with a common destiny*, then we're lost. (pp. 379–380)

For these teachers the experience was shaped by each teacher's sense of mission and commitment to children of color. Race was an aspect of their experience that cannot be underestimated or ignored. Race caused these teachers to perceive an almost familial bond with their students. At several levels, the shared cultural heritage superseded present-day social class differences. And yet, these teachers were a product of schools that, while racially segregated, were nonetheless important institutions within the Black community. The institutions where these two teachers presently work are still predominantly segregated, but their importance to the community is compromised by a perceived lack of effectiveness, and the children they described seemed to represent a "forgotten" underclass who had few connections to "the American dream" celebrated by earlier generations of middle- and working-class families.

CONCLUSION

In summary, these teachers are perhaps no different from other teachers, except that rather than internalizing a sense of failure and hopelessness tied to the school failure of large numbers of their students, they felt challenged and invigorated by the "fight." They did, indeed, perceive themselves as different from other teachers, perhaps even marginalized, but the difference could not be attributed to a single factor, but rather to a compilation of behavior, attitudes, values, and beliefs. As stated earlier, perhaps these teachers should be treated as a special category, a subculture of the larger group of teachers generally. Several common themes characterized the interviews of these teachers, but, simply stated, these teachers accepted the challenge to teach at-risk kids because of the satisfaction they experienced working in school environments characterized by a high degree of failure.

School failure is never simple; in fact, any discussion of "failure" requires predefined measures of "success" that emerge as cultural markers of status and prestige. One could propose, as does Erickson (1984), "that children failing in school are working at achieving that failure" (p. 539). Students who fail to succeed in school may be withholding their assent to these predefined notions of success and failure, and thus rejecting the accoutrements of middle-class status and prestige. Thus viewed, these teachers were engaged in a struggle to overcome overwhelmingly strong forces that make school failure a viable (and reasonable) option for some students. While I have little evidence that these teachers deliberately involved their students in a critical discourse designed to help the students better understand the choices they made, I have every reason to believe that at a personal, introspective level these teachers were engaged in a critical discourse about the choices *they* were making each day in the classroom. All of these teachers clearly believed in the innate worth and value of the work they were doing in schools and intuitively understood that it is wrong simply to talk of "student" failure; it blames the victim. McLaren (1994) discusses the tendency of many educators to "psychologize" student failure:

> This attitude is particularly frightening because teachers often are unaware of their complicity in its debilitating effects. Psychologizing school failure is a part of the hidden curriculum that relieves teachers from the need to engage in pedagogical self-scrutiny or in any serious critique of their personal

roles within the school, and the school's role within the wider society. In effect, psychologizing school failure indicts the student while simultaneously protecting the social environment from sustained criticism. (p. 216)

The teachers who participated in this study regularly scrutinized and critiqued their roles and responsibilities in relation to school failure. Specific insights gained from these reflections produced differences in the style and substance of each teacher's instruction, and yet the net outcomes were similar. Their discussions of school failure were shaped by a shared sense of mutual responsibility for that failure. These beliefs shaped the individual philosophies of these teachers and ultimately the way they viewed the aims and purposes of the teaching/learning process within the context of schools and communities.

If one treats the students discussed by these teachers as an at-risk population that represents an oppressed group who through school failure remain disenfranchised and without access to the power and status associated with educational credentials, these stories begin to fit into a larger theoretical framework. By committing themselves to the success of these students, these teachers have refused to accept the school failure of less advantaged students as the status quo; they have reconfigured the "normal" parameters of their roles and responsibilities as teachers. Their relationships with students have become *both* personal and professional, emotional as well as intellectual. They have questioned the "taken for granted assumptions" concerning school failure and have committed themselves (and their students) to a course of individual action. If "social change is a product of human action," as Giroux (1988) would argue, these teachers may be instrumental in changing the personal histories of these students by facilitating their successful navigation of the public school terrain (cited in Spring, 1994, p. 29).

Too often, what we do in classrooms is simply cultural imposition and assimilation. The relationship is one-sided, but the sword is double-edged; fail in school and fail in life. This doesn't have to be the reality, but too often it is. In many ways these students have failed only to have a constituency that counts. They have no supporters who possess the skills of negotiation, and the power and status associated with middle-class membership, to voice support for alternative visions of success and "the good life." Teachers who care may be the most powerful advocates for the rights of these students. Weiler (1988) discusses Freire's beliefs concerning "the need for teachers to respect the consciousness and culture of their students and to create the pedagogical situation in which students can articulate their understanding of the world" (Freire, 1973, p. 56; cited in Weiler, 1988, p. 18). The concept of *scaffolding* (Wood, Bruner, & Ross, 1976) has been used to describe the social relations inherent in the constitution of learning tasks. This concept seems to convey the reciprocity inherent to the teaching/learning process discussed by these teachers. Erickson (1984) utilized this important concept:

> The scaffolding relationship between teacher and learner is jointly constructed. The child has rights to ask for a range of kinds of help. . . . The child and the teacher have rights to redefine the task as part of the scaffolding negotiation. This social form of learning environment in everyday teaching situations is very different from that found in school learning environments. There, typically, the learner has much less right to help shape the task. In such a situation it may be that very often the teacher's one-sided attempts to construct a scaffold that reaches the learner don't work. The scaffold doesn't reach. (p. 533)

The value of the "scaffolding" metaphor lies in its emphasis on the interconnectedness of the teaching/learning enterprise. Ladson-Billings (1994) also uses this metaphor to describe the work of teachers:

> When teachers provide instructional "scaffolding," students can move from what they know to what they need to know . . . students are allowed (and encouraged) to build upon their own experiences, knowledge, and skills to move into more difficult knowledge and skills. Rather than chastise them for what they do not know, these teachers find ways to use the knowledge and skills the students bring to the classroom as a foundation for learning. (p. 124)

As an ideal, could it be posited that teaching and learning should be akin to a dance—equal partners, one part skill and one part art? Such a dance requires a reciprocity and interconnectedness of action in order to be successful. And such a dance, when successful, involves perfect synchronicity. But even in the most difficult circumstances, it is a relationship in which for a moment each partner shares responsibility for the outcome. Using this metaphor, the voices of both students and teachers must be woven into a rich tapestry of meaning. Truly, if we are to understand the experience of failure, the voices of both students and teachers must be heard.

Failure is reciprocal and all-encompassing; it includes both student and teacher, classroom and community, school and family. School failure will never be eliminated; it will always be with us. Yet, it would seem that some teachers and students have found ways to successfully negotiate and reconcile "typical" notions of school success and failure and to realize and subvert the political and bureaucratic mechanisms that sustain their narrow definitions. And this is as it should be. School failure should not exist in any form. Why would anyone choose to fail? What need does it meet? It would seem that every human being has an evolutionary predisposition to succeed, and perhaps they do succeed when it is deemed important to their basic survival. Listening to the teachers in this study is just one attempt to better understand this interface between success and failure.

How can this information be used to shape the experiences of preservice and inservice teachers? It seems imperative that teachers be prepared to work with students who are at risk of failing. Schools characterized by high levels of failure soon may outnumber their more successful counterparts in the suburbs. New teachers often shy away from these environments out of fear and ignorance. And, who can blame them? Who of us would seek out an opportunity to greet "failure" on a daily basis in a classroom? If demographic projections are accurate, we must acquaint large numbers of new teachers with the cognitive and pedagogical strategies that will enable them to be successful in these schools. Successful role models who are enthusiastic and excited by this challenge are a good beginning. Cochran-Smith (1991) conceptualizes this process:

> Working to reform teaching or what can be thought of as *teaching against the grain*, is not a generic skill that can be learned at the university and then "applied" at the school. Teaching against the grain stems from, but also generates, critical perspectives on the macro-level relationships of power, labor, and ideology—relationships that are perhaps best examined at the university—where sustained and systematic study is possible. But teaching against the grain is also deeply embedded in the culture and history of teaching at individual schools and in the biographies of particular teachers and their individual or collaborative efforts to alter curricula, raise questions about common practices, and resist inappropriate decisions. These relationships can only be explored in schools in the company of experienced teachers who are themselves engaged in complex, situation-specific, and sometimes losing struggles to work against the grain. (p. 280)

The voices of the teachers described in this chapter are the voices of one small group of people attempting to "teach against the grain." Their stories are incomplete. We can only assume and hope that they will not waiver in their desire and commitment to continue this effort. Teachers who are willing to teach against the grain must become the norm rather than the exception in schools where failure is pervasive. As teachers become more involved in the day-to-day decision making and planning that govern their lives, I believe that there will be a place in schools for the dialogue and sharing that are prerequisites for a critical examination of teaching and learning communities.

The most notable finding in this study is the insight these teachers provide about the experience of teaching in schools characterized by high levels of failure. It is not possible or even pragmatic to consider trying to teach novice teachers the cognitive strategies or philosophical shifts shared by these individuals. However, the teachers portrayed in this chapter are powerful reminders of those behaviors that cannot be measured or accounted for in classrooms by looking at test scores or dropout rates, or even teacher performance appraisal instruments. The overall complexity of the teaching/learning enterprise frequently is underestimated, and the tremendous energy, both physical and mental, required to teach each day often is ignored. No teaching assignment is easy, but some are more difficult than others. The information provided by the teachers in this study does not lead to specific recommendations for changes in teacher preparation or staff development; however, the importance of collaboration with teachers who are successful in the most difficult teaching assignments is reaffirmed.

A larger question concerns the establishment of schools that facilitate critical discourse among teachers about teaching and learning, success and failure, and ultimately the tenuous relationship between public schools and the needs of society. Beane and Apple (1995) write:

> The educational landscape is littered with the remains of failed school reforms, many of which failed because of the social conditions surrounding the schools. Only those reforms that recognize these conditions and actively engage them are likely to make a lasting difference in the lives of the children, educators, and communities served by the schools. . . . Democratic educators seek not simply to lessen the harshness of social inequities in school, but to change the conditions that create them. (p. 11)

School failure is unacceptable. However, it is just as unacceptable that in a country as powerful and wealthy as the United States, there are children who live in a vicious cycle of poverty and hopelessness. It seems untenable to talk about school failure without considering the circumstances that characterize the lives of those children who fail. When any one student fails, we all fail to some extent. Is the success of *all* students important? If the answer is yes, and I believe that it must be if we are to uphold the democratic ideal of equality of opportunity, the voices of good and successful teachers—those who succeed in the most challenging environments—must be included in our efforts to create democratic schools where teachers purposefully work to provide equality of educational opportunity *and* excellence for *all* children in *all* communities.

REFERENCES

Ayers, W. (1994). To teach: The journey of a teacher. *Democracy & Education, 8*(3), 9–12.

Beane, J. A., & Apple, M. W. (1995). The case for democratic schools. In M. W. Apple & J. A. Beane (Eds.), *Democratic schools* (pp. 1–25). Alexandria, VA: Association for Supervision and Curriculum Development.

Cochran-Smith, M. (1991). Learning to teach against the grain. *Harvard Educational Review, 61*(3), 279–307.

Cuban, L. (1989). The "at-risk" label and the problem of urban school reform. *Phi Delta Kappan, 70*(10), 780–801.

Dougherty, K., & Hammack, F. (1990). General introduction. In K. Dougherty & F. Hammack (Eds.), *Education & society: A reader* (pp. 1–11). Fort Worth: Harcourt Brace Jovanovich.

Erickson, F. (1984). School literacy, reasoning, and civility: An anthropologist's perspective. *Review of Educational Research, 54*(4), 525–546.

Erickson, F. (1986). Qualitative methods in research on teaching. In M. C. Whitrock (Ed.), *Handbook of research in teaching* (3rd ed., pp. 119–161). New York: Macmillan.

Farrell, E. (1990). *Hanging in and dropping out: Voices of at-risk high school students.* New York: Teachers College Press.

Foster, M. (1993). Educating for competence in community and culture: Exploring the views of exemplary African-American teachers. *Urban Education, 27*(4), 370–394.

Freire, P. (1973). *Education for critical consciousness.* New York: Seabury Press.

Giroux, H. (1988). *Schooling and the struggle for public life: Critical pedagogy in the modern age.* Minneapolis: University of Minnesota Press.

Greene, M. (1985). The role of education in democracy [Special Issue]. *Educational Horizons, 63,* 3–9.

Half of Black, Hispanic children may be poor by 2010. (1993, November 3). *Education Week,* pp. 3, 11.

High percentage of female high school dropouts quit because they are pregnant. (1994, September 14). *Asheville Citizen-Times,* p. 6A.

Hilty, E. B. (1987). *Moonlighting teachers: A thematic analysis of personal meanings.* Unpublished dissertation, University of Tennessee, Knoxville.

Kohn, A. (1991). Caring kids: The role of schools. *Phi Delta Kappan, 72*(7), 496–506.

Kvale, S. (1983). The qualitative research interview: A phenomenological and a hermeneutical mode of understanding. *Journal of Phenomenological Psychology, 14,* 171–196.

Ladson-Billings, G. (1994). *The dreamkeepers: Successful teachers of African American children.* San Francisco: Jossey-Bass.

Lieberman, A., & Miller, L. (1990). *The social realities of teaching.* In K. Dougherty & F. Hammack (Eds.), *Education & society: A reader* (pp. 193–204). Fort Worth: Harcourt Brace Jovanovich.

McLaren, P. (1994). *Life in schools: An introduction to critical pedagogy in the foundations of education.* New York: Longman.

Ogbu, J. (1990). Social stratification and the socialization of competence. In K. Dougherty & F. Hammack (Eds.), *Education & society: A reader* (pp. 390–401). Fort Worth: Harcourt Brace Jovanovich.

Schubert, W. H. (1991). Teacher lore: A basis for understanding praxis. In C. Witherell & N. Noddings (Eds.), *Stories lives tell: Narrative and dialogue in education* (pp. 207–233). New York: Teachers College Press.

Spring, J. (1994). *Wheels in the head: Educational philosophies of authority, freedom, and culture from Socrates to Paulo Freire.* New York: McGraw-Hill.

Swadener, E. B. (1990). Children and families "at-risk": Etiology, critique and alternative paradigms. *Educational Foundations, 4*(4), 17–39.

Wehlage, G. (1993). Social capital and the rebuilding of communities. In *Issues in restructuring schools* (Report No. 5). Madison: University of Wisconsin, Center on Organization and Restructuring Schools

Weiler, K. (1988). *Women teaching for change: Gender, class & power.* Granby, MA: Bergin & Garvey.

Witherell, C., & Noddings, N. (1991). Prologue: An invitation to our readers. In C. Witherell & N. Noddings (Eds.), *Stories lives tell: Narrative and dialogue in education* (pp. 1–12). New York: Teachers College Press.

Wood, B., Bruner, J., & Ross, G. (1976). The role of tutoring in problem solving. *Journal of Child Psychology and Psychiatry, 17,* 89–100.

CHAPTER 5

From Our Voices: Special Education and the "Alter-Eagle" Problem

SUSAN J. PETERS, ALAN KLEIN, & CATHERINE SHADWICK

Between me and the other world there is ever an unasked question, "How does it feel to be a problem?"
— W. E. B. Du Bois, "Strivings of the Negro People"

Writing a century ago, the noted African American sociologist W. E. B. Du Bois felt the oppression of marginality in American society as both a gift and a curse. In 1991, an African American high school student from the "other world" of special education echoes Du Bois's feelings of oppression: "Everyone has problems and alter-eagles [*sic*] to maintain.[1] And mine is to succeed in life and not let anyone else be pulling me down." Du Bois's question—"How does it feel to be a problem?"—is still unasked today of the 4,000,000 students labeled as learning disabled (LD) in American schools and shunted off to special education classes where they are reminded in small and large ways every day that they are a problem. The reminders manifest themselves in jeers from other students who call them "loco-dummies," in embarrassing announcements over the school intercom system ("Will the 'special ed' students please report for their field trip"), and in the school counselor's belief in the "superiority of grouping students according to ability," with the subsequent low expectations that the students feel acutely.

This chapter relays the thoughts and feelings of approximately 40 students (mostly male) with learning disabilities in an urban high school composed almost entirely of African Americans. Labeled as learning disabled early in school—most by third grade—these students have spent the majority of their lives in segregated classrooms under the auspices of special education programs. They have come to see themselves as failures and are perceived by others as having failed to meet the standards of a regular education.

As the three authors of this chapter came to know these students over a period of 3 years (20 years for the special education teacher), our own lives were transformed. We felt frustrated in our mostly ineffectual attempts to change the system that we felt devalued and at best forgot to include these students once they were shunted off to special education classes. We came to believe that their voices are essential to developing an understanding of the effects of being labeled and put in special classes: high dropout rates, personal disillusionment, and disenfranchisement. As one student put it, "A lot of kids want to come [to school] but no one cares."

"Alter-eagles" is an apt metaphor for these students' struggles, particularly in American society. The eagle is our national symbol of majesty, freedom, and power. The eagle soars, makes its nests in the highest trees, and reigns supreme over its natural environment. In today's society, the eagle is also an endangered species, its natural habitat increasingly encroached upon. Many students with learning disabilities strive to develop an alter-ego that embodies the symbolism inherent in the eagle. However, like the eagle, their self-image is endangered by the conditions of schooling in today's society.

As we listened to these students—in class discussions, in informal conversations, and through self-expression in journal writing, poetry, and writing assignments—we realized that their voices provide a powerful counterpoint to the root paradigm of disability as innate individual deficiencies inherent in special education. Specifically, special education is based on the belief that (1) disability is biologically based; (2) disabled persons face endless problems that are caused by the impairment; (3) disabled persons are "victims"; (4) disability is central to the disabled person's self-concept and self-definition; and (5) disability is synonymous with a need for help and social support (Fine & Asch, 1988).

In contrast to this root paradigm, what emerged for us was a picture of resilient students who had come to view their task in school as maintaining their self-respect. These students are not only survivors by way of remaining in school; we believe they have developed a concept of themselves that enables them to skillfully manage a system that has largely failed to understand them or to meet their needs. Masten (1994) defines resilience as "successful adaptation despite risk and adversity" (p. 3). Taylor (1994) proposes a similar definition of resilience as a "display of adaptive behavior despite risks and adversities" (p. 119). However, risk and adversity are defined in the literature on resiliency mainly in terms of socioeconomic status, exposure to crime, and minority status (i.e., factors outside of school). Adaptation mainly refers to school norms and expectations. In contrast, the voices of students with learning disabilities in this urban high school reveal significant in-school conditions that put students at risk as well. Essentially, the students' perspectives that follow pose the following questions regarding these definitions: Adaptation to what? Successful in whose terms?

In the final analysis, our story is not complete in the sense that we do not attempt to explain the cause of these students' failure to thrive in school, or to argue moral imperatives. We also know very little about their lives outside of school except for what they chose to share. Our goal in presenting the voices of the students themselves is not to condemn, but to illuminate. We merely ask the fundamental question, "How does it feel to be a problem?" We believe that if more educators asked themselves and students this question, we would begin to see a paradigm shift toward the view of disability as a social construction and toward the development of a school environment that begins to see the "problem" in terms of school culture, expectations, and opportunities to learn rather than in terms of deficient students.

INTERPRETIVE CONTEXT—THE IMPORTANCE OF SELF-REVELATIONS THROUGH CRITICAL PEDAGOGY

Although we collected a lot of "hard" data (course grades, standardized test scores, absentee rates) over the course of our experiences, as we analyzed the data it became evident to us that discourse was central to our inquiry into the lives of students. Our notes and observations contained a great deal of discourse among ourselves and with students. We needed to understand students through a process of self-introspection as well as through interpretation of student voice. Examining our discourse is necessary to problematize the concrete experiences expressed through student discourse. The act of problematizing produces a dialectic between reflection and action that leads to deeper understanding. This analysis of discourse and its method of problematization is central to critical pedagogy. "Problematization is not only inseparable from the act of knowing, but also inseparable from concrete situations" (Freire, 1996, p. 153).

To imagine how it feels to be a problem requires a self-conscious effort. Even though we may feel empathy, by virtue of our roles, we are an inherent part of the establishment, part of the problem. Therefore, it seemed necessary for us to look behind our roles through examining both our own inner dialogue and the student talk that ultimately shapes our roles. We hope that, by doing so, we may develop "alter-eagles" as well. For what these students want for themselves is ultimately what we all strive for—to develop a sense of dignity, pride, respect, and power. To soar like the eagle.

This chapter, then, attempts to reconstruct students' dialogue with the aim of creating a new discourse surrounding the meaning of disability. This approach is at heart an examination of ideas and attitudes from a theoretical base. We draw from a self-conscious examination of our experiences and take the talk that constitutes our data to build a discourse faithful to student voices, while at the same time framing it theoretically. We take the stance that "if pedagogy is to address 'the transformation of consciousness that takes place in the intersection of three agencies—the teacher, the learner and the knowledge they together produce,' then education must invite genuine questions and multiple answers" (Cohen, 1993, p. 290).

The essence of our theoretical approach to learning is found in the literature on "critical pedagogy," which is defined as "working toward a critical understanding of the world and one's personal relationship to that world" (Deever, 1990, p. 71). The goal of critical pedagogy is "to help students begin to think for themselves and understand the social and moral implications of their beliefs and choices" (Deever, 1990, p. 71). Translated into classroom practice, students are encouraged to think critically, to use their personal experience to inform their writing, and to raise their awareness. Critical pedagogy succeeds to the extent that students exhibit personal growth and schools advance the notion of human justice. Specifically, "Success as a critical educator is measured by the accumulated amount of political, social and personal awareness each student takes from the class, not by the number of converts" (Deever, 1990, p. 71). Critical pedagogy is particularly apt in the context of this study, because we interacted with these students through the medium of course content in Cathy's language arts classes for students with learning disabilities, and employed the techniques of a cognitive writing strategy in our teaching of this course.[2]

Finally, and perhaps of most significance, critical pedagogy recognizes the fact that all discourses have embedded values and embodied beliefs. Although W. E. B. Du Bois did not use the term *critical pedagogy* in "Strivings of the Negro People" (1897), he exemplified the goal of critical pedagogy in his recognition that not facts, but their interpretation would induce people toward social justice. He believed that "the cure [for social inequity] wasn't simply telling people the truth, it was inducing them to act on the truth. It was not enough to determine truth scientifically; it had to be implemented politically" (Lewis, 1993, p. 226). As a result, his writing commingled advocacy with scholarship—a strategy we employ in our attempt to create a new discourse regarding students with learning disabilities.

Any theory, critical pedagogy included, is only as good or as bad as the way it is interpreted and used in practice. In this study, critical pedagogy is used to give individuals the basis for confronting values and experiences, and to raise the consciousness of ourselves and others with regard to attitudes and beliefs about disability that have not been examined carefully. A dialogue among scholars/students that focuses on questions of disability practices in special education holds the possibility of raising awareness and liberating us from past conceptions and actions that have led to student failure.

Critical pedagogy is not without its critics. Elizabeth Ellsworth (1989) argues that critical pedagogy fails to empower people because it incorrectly assumes equal power relations (between students and teachers) and its principles rest on the "Utopian" ideal that "all ideas are tolerated and subjected to rational critical assessment against fundamental judgments and moral principles" (p. 314). While critical pedagogy needs to attend to the issues of imbalances in authority that Ellsworth raises, its inherent focus on a dynamic praxis involving growth, change, and interdependence of thought with action provides the tools and, at least, the opportunity for empowerment.

Because our interactions with students represent different professional roles (graduate student, university professor, classroom teacher), and embody different lenses we bring to interpreting our interactions with students, it is important to begin our analytical discourse by providing some sense of our own perspectives and motives that we bring to school. Our first impressions upon entering the high school reveal a great deal about ourselves and the school context.

As a graduate student in school psychology with a master's degree in guidance counseling, Alan focuses on students' career goals. Although from a White, middle-class background, Alan came to this urban high school with experience in substance abuse treatment and with students from homes typical of the students in this high school: nontraditional family units with histories of abuse and alcoholism. Alan is accustomed to working at the school level, scheduling students for classes, or on a one-to-one basis, testing and counseling for career choices. After spending some time observing in Cathy's language arts classes, he saw the need for providing guidance in these areas and worked with the students for several months, conducting a Self-Esteem Inventory and Career Goals Interview with each student, followed by the development of individualized career portfolios and personalized post-school plans. Alan has a young son with a severe bilateral hearing loss who will soon start primary school with special education needs, so his interest includes a personal dimension. As a novice, Alan's first impressions focused on the environment:

> I was struck by the general atmosphere of the school. The locked rooms, security staff, and lack of opportunities for students to use the library and playing fields during free time all contributed to an impression that the school was under siege.

Alan returns to this impression frequently in his dialogues with students, looking for ways to "combat" course scheduling woes and what he sees as the problem of "reaching" for life goals.

As a university professor, Susan teaches courses in special education and teacher education, among them a course entitled "Diverse Learners in Multicultural Perspective." She has taught in the barrio in East Los Angeles and in international schools abroad. Although White and middle class, she has spent a considerable amount of time in East and Southern Africa, working with disability groups on education issues; she is herself disabled and a wheelchair user. Over the course of her professional and personal experiences, she has developed a deep commitment to equity and social justice issues for disabled and African American youth. During the first 6 months at this urban high school, Susan immersed herself in classroom life and worked with a small number of students labeled as learning disabled on a creative writing project.[3] Following are her impressions from one initial observation in a general education classroom:[4]

> The room was very noisy (although several students were sleeping with their heads down on their desks). It echoed like a tin drum. At one point, one of the boys got up and did a Michael Jackson imitation from his new video. It struck me that the noise seemed to ebb and flow like waves or music, complete with crescendos and d.c. al codas. Black English is hard for me to understand—the pace is very different from my own spoken English. As usual, I was feeling overwhelmed by the end of the day.

Susan's feelings contained a mixture of fascination and fear: fascination with the energy students exhibited, and fear for her ability to channel this energy in ways that would promote student learning. This first impression of school as a dynamic milieu of rhythms and cadences would be one she capitalized on in her teaching of creative writing to these students.

One general education teacher commented that "teaching in this school is like going five rounds with Muhammad Ali every day." In contrast, as a full-time special education teacher, over the years Cathy developed a sense of her role as nurturer. She became case worker, surrogate mother, confidante, mediator. She distributes money, food, advice, and comfort in liberal doses. Cathy worries about "her students" and is constantly searching for ways to motivate them through her stress on curriculum relevant to their experiences and aspirations, as well as through teaching compatible learning styles. She values honesty and hard work and conveys these values through her content and teaching style. The act of teaching, for Cathy, conveys more of a sense of ritual in its positive sense—that of psychosocial integration in school culture.[5]

If school is a cultural terrain marked by contest and struggle, as in the "rounds with Muhammad Ali," then Cathy personifies the referee, the trainer, and the coach. She encourages her students to bear up under their pain and to search for meaning by emphasizing expressive dimensions of students' lives. She uses cooperative learning as a teaching strategy, "not only for academics, but to create a better social climate that can help the students learn skills of compromise and cooperation on the streets to avoid fighting."

Cathy's dialogue characteristically focuses on students' lives beyond the confines of school life. Although she is White, she has lived most of her life in the same neighborhoods as her students, and her husband works for the same employer as many of her students' parents.

STREET-WISE PHILOSOPHERS, IMAGE-MAKERS, AND JAZZ IMPROVISATIONISTS

Together, the authors' backgrounds described above bring diverse and authentic experiences relevant to understanding and interpreting these students' voices. As we reviewed student discourses, three patterns of responses to the "problem" of disability in the lives of these students began to emerge. We define these patterns through the use of metaphors. The first metaphor characterizes students as street-wise philosophers trying to make sense of learning disability and its influence on their lives in school. The second metaphor sees students as image-makers who manage the double image of how others see them in relation to their own view of learning disability. The third metaphor takes music as its central theme, viewing students (and ourselves) as jazz improvisationists in the quest for translating the dirge of special education status into a flexible song script with an up-beat jazz tempo. All three metaphors reveal the task of students as developing their self-respect and self-acceptance in the face of formidable odds. Their dialogue sets the stage for a new discourse, which we turn to in the final section.

The Learning Disabled Student as Street-Wise Philosopher

In addressing the question, How does it feel to be a problem?, Susan began by asking the students what the label "learning disability" meant to them in concrete terms and why they thought they had been labeled as learning disabled. She encouraged them to reflect on these questions through creative writing and in their journals as well as in class discussion. During in-class conversations, their responses to the meaning of learning disability included "behavior problems," "attitude problems," and, as one student succinctly put it, "we're slow." As to why they had been labeled, the connection to the first question was evident in responses such as, "I refused to do the work in regular ed," and "I missed a bunch of days and got behind." These students' perceptions echo a small but growing body of evidence that views learning disability as the result of poor teaching and of a system increasingly unwilling to accept students who do not fit the expectations and structure of "typical" students in the "regular" classroom.[6]

The important aspect of these views reveals itself in terms of consequences, or the ways in which students internalize or philosophize this professional view of them as behavior problems or slow learners. If we look behind the surface explanation provided by these students, we find a rich texture of multiple interpretations in their writing.

To begin with an understanding of the consequences surrounding learning disability as a label, students further defined it in terms of their relations with others. In their writing, students adamantly and clearly articulated perceptions others held toward them and the status this conveyed: "A lot of people think that people in LD are out of their minds. They think that people in LD can't do nothing for themselves. They have names for you—Retarded, Backward, Idiot. They think special ed is for dummies." Students conclude that "a lot of people don't know what LD is all about." To these students with learning disabilities, special education means extra help, special attention. From their perspective, being labeled LD and attaining special education status is a short-term solution to their learning problems. As one student put it, "I figured I needed help on math so I would learn my times tables and get out [of special education]—that's it." They believe that "all students should be treated the same way" and that "no matter if we are in special classes, we should all be learning on the same level."

Their view of others' misperceptions makes them angry. They feel a deep sense of injustice: "It's just not right because I think that the next person is no better than me." Many of the students' responses to being perceived as "dummies" reveal an inner strength buoyed by this anger. As one student put it, when people put her down, "I come to reality and say, 'Ain't nobody perfect. You're learning like everybody else.'" This inner dialogue displays a self-encouragement that shows through frequently in student journal writing, as in the following excerpt: "Dummies become good learners. I'm going to succeed in a lot of things like graduating, going to college, and getting a good job that will support me and mines." Their street-wise philosophy epitomizes itself in one student's admonition: "Times are going to get hard, but look to the top. Never give up and you'll make it."

In getting "to the top," these students know what they want and what they need to get there. From their Career Goals Interview, Alan found that most of these students look toward a college education. When he asked, "What is the one thing that will help you achieve your career goals," they cited specific coursework to help them attain needed skills, and specific strategies such as working with their counselor. Most students also stressed values of hard work, determination, motivation, patience, responsibility, and self-confidence. They know the barriers they face, which for most of them include dropping out of school (approximately 50% each year). The second most frequent barrier they cited is drugs. One teenager listed "death" as the one thing that could keep him from reaching his goal.

Violence and death are a reality of life all teenagers at this high school often face. One local news headline during the school year asked, "Padlock Latest School Weapon?" The article began with the following: "School officials have concentrated on ridding buildings of guns and knives, but a new weapon has been blamed in an assault against a high school student— a padlock." A follow-up article carried the following headline: "Schools Plan Hot Line for Ideas to Stem Violence." In the face of school violence, the student's admonition to "never give up" gives a new meaning to "at risk" and forces the question: What are schools for?

Given these barriers, the distance between knowing what they want and getting it often seems very far. But many students still put their faith in schooling, despite their status as "dummies" and their potential for being at risk for dying, let alone school failure. For several students, special education is a key to success: "I like special attention. That's what most people, especially ones with emotional problems need. I know most regular students want that but can't get it [in 'regular' education]."

Although they recognize the value of individual attention in school, students puzzle over the fact that they must be labeled to get this attention. Their acknowledgment of this dilemma is poignant and instructive: "I feel that people shouldn't label other people, because they don't like to be labeled themselves. If more people would think about how it feels to be called a name or put in categories, they would know how it feels to be called a name. I think that it is about time someone told them that there is no difference between us." This student's reflections get at the heart of how it feels to be a problem, and raise serious questions regarding the value of labeling.

Overall, these students' street-wise philosophy reveals a great deal of strength in the face of psychological violence to their images. Their insights show a sense of injustice that they combat through an inner dialogue consisting of reality checks ("Ain't nobody perfect") and self-encouragement ("Never give up and you'll make it"). These students' street-wise philosophy uncovers the thought processes by which students develop and maintain self-respect, but how do they outwardly manage their relations with other students and teachers in school? We found a depth of sophistication in students as image-makers.

Image-Making as a Juggling Act

One student provided a telling insight on the ability to juggle the consequences of being labeled learning disabled: "Labeling makes you one of two things: weak or strong." Labeling is a process of testing and diagnosis that looks for deficiencies in students. From the students' perspective, turning the tables on professionals who ascribe this label to them would lead to significant changes in the system: "If you found out what they're not good at and put a label on them they would feel real low because you are messing around with their weakness. And no one wants you to play with their weakness because if it is your weakness you can say too much about it."

Many students with learning disabilities worry that other students will discover these "weaknesses." They spend a lot of energy hiding their label from friends. One student asks, "Let's say what if they found out? Would they still be my friends? Would they still go to the park with me? Or would they just blow my cover and tell everyone I was in special ed?" He decided that he didn't want to take the risk, so "it was very important that I kept my secret to myself."

One important way to keep the secret of special education status involves teachers as gatekeepers. Juggling classes is an essential part of image-making in high school. One of the easiest ways to "blow a student's cover" is management of the classroom environment. Cathy keeps the window in her classroom covered with construction paper so students passing by won't see inside because small class size is the easiest tip-off that this is a special education room. She also allows students to come and go at times other than the bell, so they won't be seen entering or leaving the classroom. Within class, seating arrangements are important ways to juggle one's image as well. In some classes, students segregate themselves by seating. One student observed: "In my class those who want to learn sit on one side of the class and those who don't want to learn sit on the other."

Class schedules also have to be juggled. Getting the courses one needs to obtain a high school diploma is a maze of interlocking steps. One senior wanted a business computer class. The prerequisite for this class is account-ing. In order to take accounting, a student must have a certain number of math credits, which if not taken prior to junior year, rules out the computer class in senior year. In addition to this maze of gatekeeping, many students take special ed and "regular" ed math, special ed language arts and "regu-lar" ed language arts. They get further and further behind in accumulat-ing required credits for graduation if they don't learn the juggling act of course-taking sequences early in high school. And this juggling act, which is difficult for all students, is particularly so for special education students.

Some students can't see any way out. They give up trying to juggle. Encouraged to put her feelings into writing, one such teenager who had given up composed the following "rap" poetry:

BEAT UP

There are some people
that just beat you any kind of way,
no matter who you are
or what classes you are in.
There are those who think that they're better than you
and those who treat you special
and those who think
you can't do anything right. (Sekesai)

These are the students Cathy worries most about, providing what indi-vidual counseling she can during the course of the day as a safety net for their pain. The line "those who treat you special" provides the single up-beat to the students' school dirge, leading to the theme of the need for flex-ibility in school for students who do not fit the mold. But getting the "spe-cial help" they need risks damage to their image. One student's essay entitled "On Special Education and the Problem with It" capsulizes this dilemma: "There are advantages and disadvantages as far as the teacher can give you the help you need, and then you have the label of being a dummy." In order to manage this dilemma, many of the students' sugges-tions take the form of improvisation. They ask, "Why not teach us like regu-lar teachers teach them [general education students] even if it takes us longer if it has to? Why not give us more learning things?"

Jazz Improvisationists

Students with learning disabilities realize they need special attention. Spe-cial education at least attempts to provide this special attention through a

flexible learning environment where general education has failed. Individu-
alizing instruction is a form of improvisation on the part of both teachers
and learners. In her field notes near the end of the school year, Susan reflects on the work of improvisation:

> Today I worked with first-hour students analyzing an article on
> apartheid. Second-hour students didn't get it because I realized first
> hour resented being pulled out and missing a movie. Third-hour
> students worked on entirely different individual work. Besides
> working on different things per class hour, each student is at a
> different level of interest and ability. What a challenge! Now I am
> beginning to understand what Cathy faces every day.

In October, Alan's reflections on his work with the students' career
planning carried the citation: "I think what is needed is structure, structure, structure." But by January, he was saying, "I think individual attention was helpful for many of the students . . . they have been working dili-
gently . . . I enjoyed processing their college plans with them individually."
Cathy's improvisation takes form in her stress on thematic units, which
enables students to activate prior knowledge and provides a conceptual
framework built from background experience to anchor the content. However difficult this task of individualization seems to teachers, students yearn
for "more learning things." Shunted off to special education classes, they
spend their subsequent lives trying to earn their way back to being "regular" again. Students find it especially difficult, though, to accept that they
are given special attention in separate classes when "there are students in
regular ed who can't learn any better than those who are in special ed." In
her 20 years of experience, Cathy supports this view, believing that most
students in this high school are struggling academically whether in general or special education: "Most students have some kind of learning disability. Some kids just happen to be given the label."
Many students' thoughts about being singled out from their peers for
this special attention are characteristic of musical rhythms and genre. For
some students, school seems like a march or a hymn with the same chorus:
repetitious and slow. Said one student, "Some teachers have us learning
out of the same book year after year, then we never have the time to learn
that much out of a regular book." Acutely aware that they are out of step
with general education classes, others find a lack of harmony, an out-of-
syncness: "Say (for example), if we both had the same book and they [regu-
lar education students] would be on page 167 and we would be on page
66. . . ." This type of improvisation creates discord. It is more like a

cacophony of sound—an orchestra with no maestro, a song with no regular beats per measure.

Still other students talk about special attention in ways reminiscent of solo performances within a main theme. "I figured I needed help on math so I would learn my times tables and get out—that's it!" However, solo performances still require a backup orchestra: "I feel that no matter if we are in special classes, we all should be learning on the same level."

What students are asking for in the above critique is learning that has a regular beat, but a faster tempo and improvises while maintaining harmony. Essentially, this entails a musical script where no part is left out, but solos are encouraged, and the range of octaves is unlimited. They want school to be a jazz session: creative, challenging, spiritual, collectively harmonized, a session that enhances and allows development of their "alter-eagles."

SCHOOLING, DISABILITY, AND THE ALTER-EAGLE SOLUTION

We wish we could say that the students whose thoughts and feelings we conveyed were successful in developing and maintaining "alter-eagles" and in attaining their career goals. Of the girls, one is working two shifts in a convalescent home, and another had a baby boy, but is taking a correspondence course and wants to attend junior college next year. One of the boys obtained a football scholarship for a midwestern university, but dropped out during the first year when his sister was killed. Another spent one semester at a local junior college, then dropped all classes but one because "it was too much work." We don't know much about the rest of the students, although several of them have returned at least once to talk with Cathy, and she gives them as much encouragement as she can.

In the beginning of this chapter, we described these students as resilient. We ascribed resilience on the surface to remaining in school despite the odds of dropping out. Behind remaining in school, we portrayed a deeper resilience—that of students who maintain their self-respect through inner dialogue as well as personal and thoughtful challenges to the school system. This view of resilience is at odds with the main body of resilience research and theory, which points to mediating variables that include effective parenting, religious faith, and socioeconomic advantages—all outside factors—with one intraindividual factor, "good intellectual skills."

From our perspective, much of the literature on resilience misses the point and passes the buck. It misses the point in that it assumes that adaptation to poor schooling should be a student's goal. It passes the buck in assuming that adaptation is to a large extent the students' and/or parents' and community's responsibility. Several teachers in this high school support this assertion in their belief that "parents assume no responsibility." From these teachers' view, "schools are only imaging the community [lack of involvement)." These teachers ask, "Why assume responsibility [for these students] when no one [especially parents] will hold you accountable?" The majority of students with learning disabilities, however, when asked who had helped them the most in working toward their career goals (Career Goals Interview), cited family members—most often their mothers. Only two students mentioned teachers as being supportive. Because these students look to their families for support, these teachers' views contrast sharply with the students' perceptions.

We began by asserting that listening to students provides an opportunity for professionals to reframe the problem from one of at-risk students (and uncaring parents) to an examination of the school context and to the creation of a new discourse centered on social construction of disability. We focused on disability issues; however, the issues these students raise challenge much of the entire field of educational reform, with its emphasis on structure and traditional forms of pedagogy that concentrate on instruction and curriculum to the exclusion of values. If one truly listens to these students' insightful analyses of special education and the problem with it, the message conveyed necessitates a dynamic praxis between theory and what goes on in schools, with a focus on values. This focus on values invites genuine questions such as, How does it feel to be a problem? We find little in the research on resilience that addresses this question. The student who said, "If more people would think about how it feels to be called a name or put in categories, they would know how it feels . . ." speaks directly to the point. And the feeling is unanimous: "It's just not right because I think that the next person is no better than me."

It has been said that the conditions at the edge of society reveal more about the state and progress of society than conditions at the middle. African American youth labeled as learning disabled are most certainly at the edge. The system of special education and the students labeled as disabled within this system convey significant values about the nature of commitment to education and the politics of schooling. Specifically, the story of these students, as revealed by their voices and experiences in an all-Black urban high school, discloses reams about the process of school failure and its long-term effects. The analysis implies that school reform must attempt more than restructuring programs and services, but also reordering priorities and re-examining student and teacher lives in classrooms. School reform efforts that ignore the lived experiences and perspectives of students and teachers in classrooms are doomed to failure just as surely as the students have failed to learn and to develop the self-esteem they need for success beyond schooling. Understanding the lives of students labeled as learning disabled and the teachers who teach them holds promise for preventing all students from acquiring "school-learning" disabilities in a dysfunctional system.

Solutions to the social, political, and ideological dilemmas that schooling poses for students with learning difficulties will not be easy. Complex problems demand critical examination of teacher and learner and the knowledge they produce *together*. We can begin with a critical self-examination of the values inherent in the practice of labeling and its consequences. At the individual level, this self-examination entails both self-criticism and a commitment to transforming existing problems inherent in school practices such as labeling and segregation into "special" classes. The inner dialogue we presented as teachers has revealed for us the necessity for what Henry Giroux (1994) terms "sensitive political and ethical roles as public intellectuals who selectively produce and legitimate particular forms of knowledge and authority" (p. 279). We have attempted to present student voice as the basis for this knowledge and authority. The transformation we speak of involves supporting students' quest for learning and self-determination.

At the macro level, the field of special education, as well as cross-disciplinary studies that include theories of resilience and critical pedagogy, might well challenge current values inherent in the view of disability as biologically based. Such a discourse centered on values that enhance student success in school necessarily takes up the themes and underlying social processes inherent in student image-making, improvisation, and development of self-respect and pride. With this discourse, we may alleviate the failures so often experienced by students with learning difficulties, and all of us involved in schools may learn, in time, to soar like the eagle.

NOTES

The authors wish to thank Doug Campbell for his insightful review and thoughtful editorial comments on this chapter.

1. The student whose quote we use here and in the chapter's title obtained the spelling of "alter-eagles" from a hand-held electronic spell-check computer that suggests alternatives to misspelled words.

2. The cognitive writing strategy employed with these students was adapted from Carol Sue Englert's extensive research with LD students. The strategy, entitled POWER, contains the following elements of creative writing: Plan, Organize, Write, Edit, Revise. We added an additional groupwork strategy, TAG: Tell what you like, Answer questions, Get feedback. See Englert (1990, 1992) and Englert et al. (1991) for sources for this approach.

3. Many of the student quotes in this chapter derive from the outcome of this project—a newsletter entitled "From Our View," which was disseminated to teachers and used in the university course, "Diverse Learners in Multicultural Perspective." The students wrote with these audiences in mind.

4. The teacher of this general education language arts class had planned a rehearsal of a play for this class session, but reverted to individual "seatwork" because the main actors were absent. Absenteeism is very high, especially on Fridays, the day that this observation took place.

5. Peter McLaren's book, *Schooling as a Ritual Performance*, is an excellent treatise reflecting conditions of schooling with particular relevance to LD students. His perspective is consonant with our meaning here: "Ritual makes symbols, metaphors and root paradigms incarnate; into enfleshed enacted meaning" (McLaren, 1993, p. xiii).

6. The view of learning disability has become so amorphous that a leading special educator asserted that 80% of all children in typical classes could be labeled as learning disabled as a result of disagreement in the field regarding the definition of learning disability (Ysseldyke, 1986).

REFERENCES

Cohen, J. (1993). Constructing race at an urban high school: In their minds, their mouths, their hearts. In L. Weis & M. Fine (Eds.), *Beyond silenced voices: Class, race and gender in United States schools* (pp. 289–308). Albany: State University of New York Press.

Deever, B. (1990). Critical pedagogy: The concretization of possibility. *Contemporary Education, 61*(2), 71–77.

Du Bois, W. E. B. (1897). Strivings of the Negro people. *Atlantic Monthly, 80,* 194–198.

Ellsworth, E. (1989). Why doesn't this feel empowering? Working through the repressive myths of critical pedagogy. *Harvard Educational Review, 59*(3), 297–324.

Englert, C. S. (1990). Unraveling the mysteries of writing through strategy instruction. In T. E. Scruggs & B. Y. L. Wong (Eds.), *Intervention research in learning disabilities* (pp. 186–223). New York: Springer-Verlag.

Englert, C. S. (1992). Writing instruction from a sociocultural perspective: The holistic, dialogic, and social enterprise of writing. *Journal of Learning Disabilities, 25*(3), 153–172.

Englert, C. S., Raphael, T. E., Anderson, L. M., Anthony, H. M., Stevens, D. D., & Fear, K. L. (1991). Making writing strategies and self-talk visible: Cognitive strategy instruction in writing in regular and special education classrooms. *American Educational Research Journal, 28,* 337–372.

Fine, M., & Asch, A. (1988). Disability beyond stigma: Social interaction, discrimination, and activism. *Journal of Social Issues, 44*(1), 3–22.

Freire, P. (1996). Extension or communication. *Education for critical consciousness*. New York: Continuum.

Giroux, H. A. (1994). Doing cultural studies: Youth and the challenge of pedagogy. *Harvard Educational Review*, *64*(3), 278–308.

Lewis, D. (1993). *W. E. B. Du Bois: Biography of a race*. New York: Henry Holt.

Masten, A. S. (1994). Resilience in individual development: Successful adaptation despite risk and adversity. In M. C. Wang & E. W. Gordon (Eds.), *Educational resilience in inner-city America: Challenges and prospects* (pp. 3–25). Hillsdale, NJ: Erlbaum.

McLaren, P. (1993). *Schooling as a ritual performance: Towards a political economy of educational symbols and gestures*. New York: Routledge.

Sekesai, (1992). Beat up. *From Our View*, *1*(1), 2.

Taylor, R. D. (1994). Risk and resilience: Contextual influences on the development of African-American adolescents. In M. C. Wang & E. W. Gordon (Eds.), *Educational resilience in inner-city America: Challenges and prospects* (pp. 119–137). Hillsdale, NJ: Erlbaum.

Ysseldyke, J. E. (1986). The use of assessment information to make decisions about students. In R. Morris & B. Blatt (Eds.), *Special education research and trends*. New York: Pergamon Press.

CHAPTER 6

Failure as Discrimination: One Professor's Response to a College-Wide Examination of Proficiency in Writing

SUSAN R. MERRIFIELD

When I was a child, I suspected that many of my teachers, particularly those who taught in junior high school, enjoyed failing kids. I pictured them sitting at cramped little desks in poorly lit rooms, gleefully and sadistically slapping Fs and Ds on report cards and papers. Yet, in my more than 20 years as a teacher, I have never experienced any pleasure in giving low or failing grades. In fact, it has been my experience that most teachers construct their courses so that few students fail. Generally, we want success—for ourselves, our students, their parents, principals, and deans, if not for our own peace of mind.

However, sometimes good grades mask failure, as was the case with a former high school honors student of mine who could not read above an elementary school level. As Delpit (1988) indicates, failure also can mask discrimination when students of color fail because of cultural conflicts and miscommunications between them and their White teachers. Likewise, Heath (1988) reveals that the cultural and language use differences between both low-income Whites and low-income students of color often make it difficult for them to experience school success with their more middle-class White teachers. Sometimes this failure comes in the form of low grades; other times failure presents itself as good grades that hide a lack of learning.

MY ALMA MATER

My story is somewhat like those that Delpit and Heath tell. Certainly it involves conflicts between cultures, as well as general questions about the meaning and control of culture. Interestingly, this tale has a beginning but no real ending. My story about the struggle to create an introductory English course that successfully teaches mostly underprepared, nontraditional undergraduates how to write and read on a college level begins in the mid-1960s, after the assassination of JFK, but before the deaths of Bobby Kennedy and Martin Luther King, Jr. Vietnam had not yet heated up, and for many the War on Poverty was still a struggle that could be won. It was in this context that my alma mater, the focus of this chapter, was born. As indicated by the June 1965 statement of purpose, the primary mission of the public college that I will call "Urban University" was to "seek out, and support, those young people whose race, or recent immigration, or depressed economic status, denies them higher education and even the expectation of it." Put most simply, Urban University, an almost open-access university in the northeast United States, was founded as a stepping stone out of poverty and failure. Yet, ironically, failure in one form or another was what most students in the first few classes encountered at this city college. Looking back now 30 years, some blame this situation on admissions policies, low funding levels, or the hotly debated classical curriculum that was taught during the first 5 years in the life of Urban University (UU).

In 1967, I became part of this experiment in classical higher education for nontraditional students. To complicate matters, this particular college was situated in a city famous for its elite private colleges, in a state long reluctant to adequately fund public higher education (Millet, 1984). Undaunted by these obvious challenges to the future financial health of any public college, let alone a costly liberal arts college, the school's founding fathers strove to create, as the 1969 yearbook indicates, "a university in the ancient tradition of Western civilization." Specifically, this commitment to tradition expressed itself in 2 years of required core courses. Taken literally, the "core" was a rigorous set of general education requirements that were instituted for the purpose of transferring the privilege of an elite education to the inner-city students attending UU. These requirements consisted of: four terms each of introductory English and natural science or mathematics, four semesters of a foreign language, two semesters each of Western civilization and social sciences, and upper-division distribution requirements of four terms outside the major division (two courses being in humanities above the introductory level).

In 1965, students who attended what was beginning to be referred to cynically as the poor man's Harvard took an introductory English course that was designed to give them an overview of the literary canon of Western civilization, from Homer's *Odyssey* and Virgil's *Aeneid* in the fall of their freshman year to the work of Joyce, Faulkner, and Yeats in the spring of their sophomore year. Students were expected to respond to these texts on a series of quizzes, examinations, and writing assignments. More often than not, they had great difficulty even understanding the language used in their assignments, such as the demand of one professor that, like Dante, they should "be vivid, violent, vindictive, and vituperative."

Roughly 20 years after my freshman year, one of the school's first administrators explained to me during a 1987 interview that he was trying to create an undergraduate experience not much different from that offered at the City College of New York (CCNY) during the 1940s and 1950s. Of that New York experience, one former student writes: "My years as a student at City College seemed to offer me a rare opportunity to learn languages, read remote literature, sense other times, other qualities of life, ruminate about other value systems, and discover the range of experience" (Freedman, 1980, p. 205).

It is probably accurate to suggest that the original mission of Urban University was to offer disadvantaged students the same opportunity for a liberal education that many now famous first-generation college students received at CCNY. In this regard, the author of UU's original mission statement believed that the university should provide education in three broad categories: (1) education for a profession, (2) education for citizenship, and (3) education for self-realization and cultural enrichment. He and the first chairman of the English Department believed that a Great Books curriculum was the most appropriate introductory English curriculum for the purposes of providing education for citizenship, cultural enrichment, and a solid academic background for the professions.

As was the case with Urban University, the creation of equal opportunity through public higher education was indeed the mission of CCNY during the 1930s, 1940s, and 1950s. However, there is one critical difference between that institution at that time and UU during the mid-1960s: CCNY had stiff entrance requirements. Students had to be well prepared for college work in order to gain admission. CCNY was "a place for motivated achievers seeking a ticket out of poverty" (CBS News, 1975). In fact, by the late 1950s, only 13% of the high school graduates in New York were able to gain admission to a city college (CBS News, 1975).

In comparison to the situation at CCNY in the 1950s, the high school backgrounds of UU's class of 1969 were very uneven. As 1965–1967 admissions data indicate, 24% of the first-year class scored between 350 and 450 on the verbal portion of the SAT. Thus, one could predict easily that many would have great difficulty with college level English courses, especially in a program that required a great deal of challenging reading. However, this seems to be the type of student whom the school's first dean anticipated. In our 1987 interview, he indicated that he did not expect that the bulk of the first class would have so much as attended a college preparatory program in high school. Nevertheless, he prescribed the Great Books curriculum taught in small classes as the best way for these underprepared students to catch up to their more privileged peers. It was not his intention that all who entered would be able to run the gauntlet—he only wanted to provide equal opportunity, as he said, "more than once if necessary," to the race. True Jeffersonians (Foerster, 1937), UU's founding fathers saw the primary mission of public higher education as developing the natural intellectual aristocrats, the guardians of democracy, among previously disenfranchised groups. In this context, society could not afford a "gentleman's D" for the poor.

Democratic educational theories aside, in the classroom, the Great Books curriculum presented an often overwhelming teaching challenge for many faculty having little experience teaching underprepared students. However, during the early years of this institution, the conflicts that developed over curriculum in no way appear to have extinguished enthusiasm and interest in the instruction of first-year English. On the contrary, the heated discussions that occurred appear to have stimulated involvement. After all, from 1965 to 1967, with the university composed of only freshmen and sophomores, faculty taught only introductory courses. The first Director of Freshman English still recalls the "missionary feeling" that he and most faculty felt. According to him, everyone knew there would be "a lot of sweat and journeyman work" involved in setting up curricula in a university that did not have a library and was housed in a few old buildings.

WITH THE NOBLEST INTENTIONS

The youthful UU faculty was, for the most part, already caught up in the rhetoric and ideals of both the War on Poverty and the antiwar movement. Therefore, they were highly motivated to influence the intellectual quality of the lives of blue-collar college students. Many refer to this early period at UU as a time of "creative chaos." Faculty did not simply moan and groan about the problems they had with the curriculum; they went to work developing both revisions of the Great Books curriculum and totally new approaches to the instruction of introductory English.

In 1967, while most members of UU's English Department were busy creating their own personal recipe for the best replacement for the classical curriculum, my own personal odyssey from object of enlightened social policy to college professor began when I literally ran into the UU Admissions Office and begged for acceptance. This action was not motivated by any particular respect for or even knowledge of this institution and its rigorous curriculum; no, I simply could no longer tolerate my dead-end job as a file clerk at a local insurance agency. UU was the only school I could walk to in the amount of time provided by my lunch hour, and it was cheap at $100 a semester. The Director of Admissions made my day on that raw autumn afternoon more than 28 years ago when he accepted me on the spot for admission to the class of 1971. I was full of joy when I returned to the office to announce that I would be leaving, not to have a baby or get married, but to go to college. At my going-away party, when asked what I wanted to be, I replied that I wanted to be a writer. But that wasn't true; I had no particular career plans. I only knew that I didn't want to be a file clerk and I did want to be an educated person, whatever that meant. In this regard, I was not at all unlike many of my fellow students.

Although I had a less than distinguished record at a local public high school, I fancied myself a writer, a reader, an intellectual. As a former class poet, I couldn't wait to sign up for the many literature courses tantalizingly described in the course catalog. My dreams of being part of a course such as "Post World War II Comic Fiction" were quickly dashed by my advisor as she glared at me from behind my transcript. I left her office feeling insecure and diminished, all but doomed to failure before I began. My dream of a magic carpet ride out of boring low-wage jobs seemed to be fading fast. She had let me know in no uncertain terms that I would be extremely lucky to survive first-year English and history, courses full of required reading by unfamiliar classical writers. I tried to summon up some enthusiasm for the Old Testament, Thucydides, Plato, Aristotle, Chaucer, Dante, Milton, Voltaire, Fielding, Rousseau, Burke, and many other all but incomprehensible writers.

The new Urban University I entered in January 1968 was housed in a few dilapidated buildings on the edge of the city's South End. The state rented these buildings while the permanent location for this urban campus was fiercely (and politically) debated. To an outsider, these dirty, dusty buildings did not look like much but they were heaven to me—that is, until I started receiving very low grades and critical comments from my professors that seemed to indicate that they considered me barely literate. But I remembered my advisor's menacing warnings about the curriculum and academic standards and decided to meet the challenge. Full of determination, I struggled with calculus, chemistry, French, Virgil, and Homer. Every C I received was won with coffee, sweat, and tears.

At the same time that my hard won Cs were finally turning into Bs, most of my new friends were either flunking or dropping out of college.

The leap between what they understood and what they were supposed to learn was too wide. Additionally, many of them did not understand how classical literature or a foreign language would get them a good job. So they left, or were forced out by low grade-point averages.

In a few years, the same issues that concerned my friends about the curriculum, lack of comprehensibility, and relevance, would be echoed by the majority of the faculty at UU, who would successfully demand the abolition of the much debated general education requirements. In 1971, the year I graduated, UU abandoned its initial commitment to the creation of a "university in the ancient tradition of Western civilization" when the faculty senate voted to abolish almost all course requirements for undergraduates except "one year of training in writing to be taken in the freshman year." This freed the mostly underprepared undergraduates from the obligation to enroll in required courses in math, science, literature, and foreign languages. It also freed faculty from the demands inherent in teaching a rigorous curriculum to students who lacked high school level literacy.

Less than a quarter of the undergraduates who attended UU in the late 1960s actually graduated. In fact, to facilitate 18% of the class of 1969 reaching graduation, the Dean had to lower the GPA required for graduation from 2.0 to 1.8.

HOMECOMING

In 1982, I returned to my alma mater to teach first-year English, a course in which, within the former classical curriculum, I had struggled to earn a C. By the late 1970s, after years of discussion about the variability of students' ability to write, the College of Arts and Sciences instituted a requirement that all undergraduates pass an examination of writing proficiency before progressing to their junior year. As an instructor of first-year English, one of my responsibilities would be to develop the writing skills demanded by this test.

In the early 1980s, my students in the College of Arts and Sciences (many of whom had graduated in the top two-fifths of their public or parochial high school classes yet scored only somewhere in the 400s on the SAT Verbal) often were overwhelmed by the requirement that they successfully complete the writing proficiency test. This examination loomed as a major obstacle on their path toward a college degree and the promise of upward mobility. These undergraduates were expected to take and pass the proficiency test by the time they had completed 60 of the 120 credits toward graduation. The test required them "to demonstrate that they could write proficiently in English." Those who failed to pass the test by this midpoint in their undergraduate career were required to take a fundamental skills course and no more than 12 additional credits. Students who had earned from 68 to 89 credits without passing the proficiency test had to have their academic schedule approved by the director of the Writing Proficiency Program in addition to taking the fundamental skills course. Those who had earned 90 or more credits without passing the test were suspended from college.

As I studied the data on failure on the writing proficiency test, it became obvious that students of color and students for whom English was a second language were overly represented. Additionally, it appeared that low-income students, in general, were more likely to fail. Because I was not at all comfortable with the prospect of aiding and abetting in providing yet another instance of rejection and possibly even discrimination in the lives of students who generally had experienced less than a fair share of success, I decided to find a way to teach my courses that would allow those students who seemed almost doomed to failure to become proficient (fluent) in the kind of writing tested by the examination. To do this, I knew I would have to provide an atmosphere of purpose, relevance, safety, and support, just the kind of atmosphere that was, for the most part, missing from the undergraduate experience that I shared with many now middle-aged adults who still cringe at the mere mention of my alma mater.

The writing proficiency test is administered four times a year. True to its name, it is billed as a measure of a student's level of writing skill. As the Manual for Students states: "You are being asked to do this because the faculty regards skill in writing as essential for advanced work in advanced classes. This proficiency is demonstrated by responding to one of two questions on a given set of readings. The answer should take the form of a relatively polished essay, seven to ten paragraphs in length." The essay questions almost always require students to integrate their own knowledge with that reflected in the readings. One such test question posed the following dilemma: "Through a vigorous campaign the World Health Organization has been successful at eliminating the disease of smallpox. Suppose that you wish to reduce the infant mortality in the U.S. through a similarly intensive program. Basing your answer on the readings in Set A, and on other relevant material if you wish, what would be the major features of your program?"

In truth, given that students are writing about a group of readings, the writing proficiency test is much more than a test of writing ability. This examination is also a measure of an undergraduate's stage of reading development, specifically the development of the ability to use reading materials. For in this test, students are asked to respond in writing to a question about a set of five readings around a specific theme.

It was clear from both the demands inherent in the questions put to the students (students are expected to synthesize information and create new knowledge) as well as the readability level of the test selections of literature that a major expectation of this particular writing test is that students can read at a stage appropriate for readers on the college level and beyond (Chall, 1983). Hence, one can say that the examination is not only a test of whether a student has attained college level writing proficiency, but also a test of whether one can read at what Chall categorizes as a Stage 5 level of reading development (the level at which one is capable of analyzing and synthesizing many perspectives on a topic and then generating an original perspective).

In a 1986 memorandum to instructors of freshman English, the Director of the Writing Proficiency Program identified four recurrent problem areas found on examinations written by those who had failed the test one or more times. The number one problem area cited should be of particular interest to those concerned about literacy-related failure on the postsecondary level. It was as follows: "a tendency to summarize each assigned article instead of answering the question. Failure to analyze and synthesize the assigned materials."

The fact that a reading-related problem was cited as the most common cause of student failure on the writing proficiency test probably will come as no surprise to most in the field of higher education. Urban University, where the average student is in his or her late twenties, is full of students described by Cross (1981) as "new" or nontraditional students. Such students are frequently from low- and moderate-income communities and/or families and, as children and adolescents, did not plan to attend college. When admitted as freshmen, these students "may test as low as the seventh or eighth grade reading level"(Chall, 1977, p. 19).

Traditionally, neither freshman English nor any other of the courses taught as general education requirements contain any specific reading instruction, as evidenced by a survey of syllabi and course descriptions. Students who perform poorly on an entry (freshman) English placement test are assigned to English 010, which is basically a remedial freshman writing course, not a remedial reading course. The departmental guidelines for freshman English consist of three pages outlining the appropriate sequence of instruction in writing. Faculty are advised that "our fundamental concern throughout the year must be with clear and effective word usage and sentence form." In English 101, faculty are encouraged to assign compositions that require students "to write from their own experience, observation, opinion and reflection." In English 102, faculty are instructed to "give more time and attention to the interpretation of academic texts and other materials and their use in writing." Although such a directive possibly could indicate some sort of reading instruction, no mention is made of the fact that many below college level readers may not know how to read these texts. The major stated goal of English 102 is the creation of a research paper "of more than six typewritten pages."

By the 1980s, most UU English instructors were aware that many of their students were weak readers. Students with reading problems were encouraged to attend noncredit reading and study skills workshops run by the Office of Academic Support. Hence, student enrollment in a reading workshop was a function of personal motivation or faculty suggestion, rather than formal requirements. Considering the informal nature of remedial reading instruction available both in and outside the freshman English courses, it seems safe to assume that many students who experienced difficulty reading college level material never made it to remedial reading instruction. While designing my courses, I decided that college level reading instruction should be integrated into the curriculum, rather than set aside as a remediation. There is mounting evidence to support this inclusive instructional approach, even in college. Remediation, in itself, often makes a student feel stigmatized and segregated. Even when such programs increase nontraditional student self-esteem and better adjustment to campus life, they often do little to improve classroom performance (Raspberry, 1994).

A LADDER TO HIGHER-LEVEL LITERACY

The series of curricular innovations that I instituted in my sections of freshman English was guided primarily by my own experience as part of a college class in which failure was the norm and my background as a successful whole language K–12 teacher. As I remembered, my peers from those early days at Urban University experienced failure not just because the assigned texts were difficult to read, but because the instruction provided failed to build bridges to understanding. Most of our professors stood before us and delivered various renditions of the type of instruction they had received at elite schools and colleges. This teaching method provided nontraditional students with few strategies for learning.

I was determined to design a course with texts that were challenging enough to prepare students for the type of reading encountered on the proficiency test, organized around a theme that adult learners could care enough about to inspire both high-level comprehension and the development and exploration of deep questions.

As a prelude to my curriculum development, I reviewed the content of previous writing proficiency examinations. In the spring of 1987, UU students could choose to be tested on readings from three different areas of inquiry: the films of Robert Altman, the failure to thrive syndrome, and homelessness in American cities. These readings were selected from scholarly works in the fields of science, medicine, social science, and the humanities. When analyzed using the Fry Readability Graph (Fry, 1977), selected readings ranged from grade 11+ to 15+ in difficulty.

As already stated, it is clear from both the demands inherent in the questions put to students on the proficiency test, as well as the readability level of the test selections, that a major expectation of the examination is that students can read at a stage appropriate for readers at a college level (grade 12+). At this level, students are capable of analyzing and synthesizing many perspectives on a topic and generating an original perspective. As *A Nation Prepared* (Task Force on Teaching as a Profession, 1986) and other recent reports on the quality of American public education indicate, this is a level of literacy attained by only a small percentage of recent high school graduates. By the mid-1980s, I understood that if students were to respond positively to the challenges created by the writing proficiency test, they had to be taught to be analytical readers, writers, and thinkers. The short pieces contained in the thematic readers commonly assigned in freshman English did not prepare students adequately for the reading demands posed by the test. The literal and one-dimensional essay questions contained in these texts did not prepare students to write and think on the many levels demanded by the test (Burns & Roe, 1992).

The course I delivered was designed to accomplish all the basic goals of English 102, including a significant amount of preparation for the writing proficiency examination. In general, my findings indicate that students who received a C+ or better in this course passed the examination on their first attempt.

Over the years, I have found that students are most engaged by a thematic approach to instruction; this appears to be just as true for first graders as it is for college students. The trick is to find the right theme, or at least a compelling and relevant theme, given the age and experiential background of the students. Selecting themes is especially difficult at UU, where the average undergraduate is 27, and a typical class contains students aged 16 to 55. In the past, attempts at developing thematic approaches to instruction appeared to flop because either they were too teacher-centered or they were developed with a focus on the issues of late adolescence, such as "the generation gap" or "exploring one's personal feelings."

The thematic focus of the last literature-based course I taught while at UU was entitled "Growing Up Below the Median Income." This unit appeared to be more engaging than my previous theme, "Poverty in America," and significantly more engaging than an earlier theme entitled "Human

Values in a High Tech World." My guess is that the plight of the roughly 25% of America's children who live in poverty is more compelling than either economic or intellectual dilemmas confronted by adults. This interest probably is reinforced by the career choices that many of my former students made in the fields of teaching, social work, nursing, and counseling, as well as the fact that many UU students are parents. Additionally, it is probably important to note that many students at UU grew up below the median income and continue to live below this line.

As preparation for the writing proficiency test and the reading and writing expectations implicit in upper-level courses, my curriculum forced both students and teacher to ask questions for which none of us had the right answer; we could only interpret and offer support for our assertions. For example, when reading Carolyn Chute's *The Beans of Egypt, Maine*, a novel about Maine's rural poor written in 1985, we did not know for sure if Earlene was a victim of incest or whether her husband Beal sought escape from poverty through death; we could only develop a thesis and offer support for our analysis. Such subjects became the focus of small-group discussion, large-group note taking, and finally formal essays. This process involved real talk about real problems concerning characters with whom the students had become familiar. Most students enthusiastically explored a full range of text-related issues because they really wanted to share new theories and literary insights. In such circumstances, it logically followed, at least for many students, that we needed to conduct research (another course requirement) in order to find out more about the lives of people like Earlene and Beal who began to manifest themselves as complicated human beings who were more than "white trash" stereotypes.

As most K–12 teachers know, whole language instruction involves the use of meaningful quality literature to teach reading, writing, researching, and thinking strategies. Over and over again, researchers observe that students are transported from vacant stares and apathetic responses to lively engagement with texts and assignments when a relevant literature-based curriculum is introduced (Atwell, 1987). It seems that children need to sink their intellectual teeth into something substantial, something they can really care about. In this regard, I reasoned that if children generally experience more success in acquiring reading competency with a move from basals to trade books (Savage, 1989), then a move from readers and anthologies to trade books probably would benefit college students, many of whom read well below grade 12+ reading level.

In the whole language approach, instruction moves away from an emphasis on basic skills to an emphasis on strategies for learning (Goodman, 1986). This feature had special appeal for me as I began to observe that many of the students at UU appeared to suffer from an overdose of instruction in basic skills. They were all too eager to copy a line out of a book as an answer to a question, or parrot a memorized sentence fragment that they did not understand, rather than ask their own questions, offer an explanation, compare and analyze several ideas, or even identify main ideas and themes. My discovery that many students had read only readers, anthologies, and textbooks, rather than "whole" books, further influenced my decision that it was time for the whole language approach to go to college.

Thinking like a whole language teacher in a college setting actually was not an enormous jump for someone who was familiar with this institution's history with the Great Books curriculum. I even discovered that some faculty were still teaching a modified version of the Great Books course with success. As with any sound whole language teaching, the glue that held these courses together was relevancy, a thematic focus, and well-constructed developmentally appropriate assignments. These few teachers were skilled at revealing to nontraditional students the sex, violence, adventure, truth, and beauty to be found in the classics.

A MEANING-CENTERED CURRICULUM FOR ADULT LEARNERS

In her landmark book on adult learning styles, Cross (1981) asserts that adults prefer learning experiences that provide them with both structure and opportunities for self-direction. Additionally, Cross notes that adults often seek out education during life transitions, such as divorce or career change, and that typically adult learners are motivated by "puzzlement or curiosity, usually about controversial issues or things that are especially important in the life of the learner" (Cross, 1981, p. 85). This means that the free-floating, open-ended assignments common in introductory English are probably inappropriate for many students at UU. Also, a loosely structured reading list that does not focus on any subject in particular is probably a poor choice for older students.

In an effort to create a literature-based course that was structured, yet provided opportunities for self-direction and learning about an interesting and controversial subject, I designed a curriculum in which students read widely from a range of high-quality fiction and nonfiction, conducted research and shared their findings, participated in student-centered discussions, and wrote and thought analytically. In brief, this all occurred in a course in which students were introduced to a wide variety of real and fictional children and young adults living in poverty. These characters appear in challenging works by Tillie Olsen, Anne Moody, Jonathan Kozol, Carolyn Chute, Frenchy Hodges, James Baldwin, and others. Among other assignments, students generated discussions and writing about the characters, analyzed the conditions of the characters' lives, analyzed authors' viewpoints, compared and contrasted characterization and thematic concerns, and conducted research on organizations, people, and historical events described in the literature.

As a final project requiring all the competencies tested by the writing proficiency examination, students completed a lengthy research assignment in which they "helped" one character encountered in the literature. They defined the relevant social problem with which the character was identified; researched the background and history of the problem (e.g., child malnutrition, illiteracy, school dropouts, teens and crime, etc.); located an organization that served people such as the character; interviewed a staff member from the organization to discover the history, mission, funding sources, and type of client served, and so on; and described how their character would interact with this agency. As the final part of this assignment, students analyzed and estimated the character's chances for success with the targeted organization based on information gained from the interview and research on the problem.

I tried to design the curriculum of "Growing Up Below the Median Income" to accommodate almost all learning styles reflected in a college classroom that included so-called at-risk students. Additionally, skills instruction traditionally reserved for remedial courses, such as understanding point of view, finding the main idea, and so forth, became part of class instruction. Students also were introduced to the range of literary forms (articles, poetry, chapters, novels, short stories, biographies, informational texts, etc.) and question types represented on the writing proficiency test. Because the range of assignments was diverse and accommodated many learning styles (McCarthy, 1987), almost everyone had the opportunity to receive some sort of an A, on either an in-class written response, an analytical essay, an interview, an oral presentation, a quiz, a mini-research assignment, a letter, a rewrite, a question design, or some other writing or speaking assignment. Perhaps this was the reason that few students withdrew after they became involved in the course, even though they quickly figured out that they had to do more reading and writing than most other students enrolled in English 102.

Traditionally, the research paper is a major obstacle in English 102, and many students withdraw or flunk, rather than write it. For years, several faculty members have responded to student failure on this assignment with proposals to make the research paper an optional assignment, rather than a course requirement. My response to the demands inherent in this admittedly challenging assignment was to dedicate a great deal of class time to making the research process understandable and accessible. Through mini-research assignments in the first part of the semester, students demystified research and actually began their final assignment. This final assignment, the "help" paper mentioned above, was an outgrowth of several smaller assignments that students completed during the semester.

Student response to my curriculum was extremely positive, even though initially many students said the course struck them as too much work. I believe that this curriculum worked because the course content provided students with a meaningful structure for the development of critical reading, writing, and thinking skills in much the same way that a thematic unit focusing on dinosaurs provides a meaningful structure for first graders to launch into a wide array of reading, writing, and data-gathering assignments on a topic that is of interest to them.

Most students, particularly older ones, can get involved with topics they already care about. In this case, it is not difficult for low- and moderate-income college students, many of whom want to be social service providers, to become motivated by an exploration of the many faces of childhood poverty in America.

Class evaluations indicated that students especially appreciated the fact that they actually learned both why research is conducted and how to write a research paper. Additionally, students said that they learned a great deal from each other, from the sharing of papers and insights into the literature, as well as the required oral report on the findings of the help assignment. In this regard, my students and I experienced the benefits of another aspect of whole language teaching—collaborative learning in a college classroom (Whipple, 1987). For over a decade, elementary teachers have observed that collaborative learning often serves to prevent the sense of isolation that often leads to failure.

The major constant in teaching this curriculum was that students responded enthusiastically to course content that at first struck them as extremely depressing or, at least, something they tried to get away from by going to college. Through the process of analyzing the causes and conditions of poverty, as well as the history of our nation's response to the poor, students began to replace their personal feelings of hopelessness and helplessness and often less-than-subtle racism and sexism (which they expressed in the first assignment on the causes of childhood poverty) with understanding and a sense of the possibility, as well as the complexity, of confronting individual and social problems. This insight into the complexity of an issue prevented most students from simply summarizing the opinions of one writer or other authority figure when asked about a particular social problem.

In this course, students were challenged to look beyond images, rhetoric, and sound bites to the kind of truth revealed in serious scholarly research and quality literature. In so doing, students not only bridged barriers created by stereotypes and made-for-TV explanations, but they also learned how to become intelligent consumers of research and other forms of literature. By acquiring the ability to synthesize material from a range of literary sources, students engaged in the kind of thinking, reading, and writing required by UU's writing proficiency examination. It has been my experience that this form of expression cannot be learned through a "task-master" teacher's drill (Waller, 1965), but rather is developed through the kind of authentic practice that has become a hallmark of whole language learning.

REFLECTIONS ON SUCCESS AND FAILURE

In the majority of cases, my whole language approach to the instruction of freshman English, as well as the choice of a course theme relevant to most first-generation college students, led to success, not failure. However, this was not always the case. When students failed my course or failed to pass the writing proficiency test, I felt frustrated. In reviewing my grades over the 6-year period in which I taught college level thematic units, I found that those who failed to complete the course with a grade of C or above most often fell into one or both of two categories, (1) adults with families who worked more than 30 hours a week, or (2) students for whom English was not their first language. It is important to note that many students who were in one of or even both of these groups did receive grades of C+ or above. In fact, some of my strongest students came from each category.

Theorists such as Goodman (1986) believe that classroom materials should facilitate authentic language learning through instruction that meets the learner at his or her present level of competence and promotes growth developmentally. In this regard, my own experience as a UU alumna allowed me to understand the culture and language background of most working-class students in a way that few other academics could. For example, I was the only English faculty member who had a regional accent! On the other hand, my cultural background and academic training did not afford me a similarly natural opportunity to teach developmentally those students who were not native speakers. I did select literature that depicted characters from a full range of cultures; but often the assignments about these readings focused on issues that appeared to resonate most strongly with native-born students, such as the individual's obligations to society and society's obligations to the individual.

Educators who practice the whole language approach generally recognize that students "need a strong background in oral language to build word meanings and sentence patterns that will support comprehension in reading" (Savage, 1994). For this reason, early childhood educators encourage book talk and storytelling (Huck, Helper, & Hichman, 1989). Similarly, my course was heavily dependent on oral participation, particularly small-group discussions in which the seeds of future essays were planted. Some limited-English speakers did benefit from the support and comfort provided by these small groups that permitted easier access to language use practice; but others remained almost barricaded behind a silence that prevented the development of the kind of oral fluency that eventually could lead them to proficient writing.

My experience with the failure of some students for whom English was a second language (ESL students) taught me a lot about myself. As a believer in educational equity, I was forced to acknowledge that I lacked the background to be an equally good teacher to all my students. This caused me pain and confusion; but from conversations with colleagues, I knew that I was not alone in my discomfort. Some recommended that I grade ESL students using separate criteria that would allow them to receive credit for the amount of effort they invested in the course as well as the amount of growth they made during the semester. Those academics who graded students on the amount of new knowledge acquired in a course discouraged me from holding ESL students to a rigid standard of written performance, saying that such a practice had a discouraging if not discriminatory effect on students.

Because the writing proficiency examination was a hurdle that all students had to pass in order to graduate, I felt that finding a way to pass students without providing adequate preparation for the writing test might make me and my students feel good in the short run but also could, in some cases, only delay inevitable failure. However, given that students did have the option of submitting a portfolio of writing samples in lieu of the examination, I was also impressed by the notion that students ought to receive some credit for ongoing growth in language learning. This lack of clarity regarding assessment of ESL students left me feeling that I had to acquire more information about effective teaching strategies for ESL students and review once more my beliefs and practices concerning curriculum and instruction.

CONCLUSION

It is interesting to compare the decisions and choices I made when confronted with the specter of student failure with the responses of the professors who taught me and my peers years before serious consideration was given to the creation of a level playing field. Those young academics of the 1960s found themselves teaching in an atmosphere where the theory of survival of the fittest prevailed. Schooled in institutions where academically unsuccessful wealthy students received polite Ds and Cs, these socially conscious teachers were extremely uncomfortable with being the agents of mass academic failure. They did not want to maintain the gauntlet through which only a small number of students could pass. By abolishing the curricular and instructional demands implicit in the general education requirements, they removed a source of personal pain for themselves and failure for their students. They believed in equality and wanted passionately to teach in a way that was less punitive and more fair. After the abolition of the classical curriculum, fewer students failed and more graduated. Yet, even I cannot tell you if this change resulted in less discrimination and greater equality for those working-class students who attended Urban University.

REFERENCES

Atwell, N. (1987). *In the middle: Writing, reading, and learning with adolescents*. Portsmouth, NH: Heinemann.

Burns, P. C., & Roe, B. D. (1992). *Teaching reading in today's elementary schools*. Princeton: Houghton Mifflin.

CBS News. (1975, April 20). *Sixty minutes*.

Chall, J. S. (1977). *Reading 1967–1977: A decade of change and promise*. Bloomington, IN: Phi Delta Kappa Educational Foundation.

Chall, J. S. (1983). *Stages of reading development*. New York: McGraw-Hill.

Chute, C. (1985). *The Beans of Egypt, Maine*. New York: Warner Books.

Cross, P. K. (1981). *Adults as learners*. Washington, DC: Jossey-Bass.

Delpit, L. D. (1988). The silenced dialogue: Power and pedagogy in educating other people's children. *Harvard Educational Review, 58,* 280–298.

Foerster, N. (1937). *The American state university*. Chapel Hill: University of North Carolina Press.

Freedman, M. (1980). CCNY Days. *The American Scholar, 49,* 193–207.

Fry, E. (1977, December). Fry's readability graph: Clarifications, validity, and extension to level 17. *Journal of Reading, 21,* 249.

Goodman, K. (1986). *What's whole in whole language?* Portsmouth, NH: Heinemann.

Heath, S. B. (1988). *Ways with words: Language, life and work in communities and classrooms*. Cambridge: Cambridge University Press.

Huck, C., Helper, S., & Hichman, J. (1989). *Children's literature in the elementary school* (5th ed.). New York: Harcourt Brace Jovanovich.

McCarthy, B. (1987). *The 4 mat system: Teaching to learning styles with right/left mode techniques*. Barrington, IL: Excel.

Millet, J. D. (1984). *Conflict in higher education*. San Francisco: Jossey-Bass.

Raspberry, W. (1994, July 5). Challenge pays off. *Boston Globe*, p. 13.

Savage, J. F. (1989). *I like to teach reading with literature but I'm afraid my pupils will miss out on skills*. Littleton, MA: Sundance.

Savage, J. F. (1994). *Teaching reading using literature*. Madison, WI: WCB Brown & Benchmark.

Task Force on Teaching as a Profession. (1986). *A nation prepared: Teachers for the 21st century*. Rochester, NY: National Center for Education and the Economy.

Waller, W. (1965). *The sociology of teaching*. New York: Wiley.

Whipple, W. R. (1987, October). Collaborative learning: Recognizing it when we see it. *AAHE Bulletin*, pp. 4–6. (ERIC Document Reproduction Service No. ED289386)

CHAPTER 7

The Micro-Politics of School, Teacher, and Student Failure: Managing Turbulence

BRIAN DeLANY

Schools are continually scrambling for order in a disorderly world. Their managers work hard to impose regularities in response to this need. Sorting and categorizing students as "successful" or "failed" is one of the regularities communities have come to expect. For students, getting the right courses and teachers is as important as teachers' access to competent students. Current research and popular opinion about schools would lead us to believe that excellent students, courses, and teachers are in short supply as an essential school resource. How is it that students get access to the courses, teachers, and schools that can help ensure their "success" or brand them as "failed"? At the same time, which teachers and schools have access to "successful" students? This chapter considers how the pool of students, courses, and teachers is managed and eventually matched. The consequent labels and categorization of "success" or "failure" are seen to flow from this managed agenda of choices and selections. As the chapter will point out, for many students and teachers the labels of "success" or "failure" may result from student, teacher, or course matches that are often capricious, unintentional, or irrelevant to the educational interests of the participants.

From the beginning of each year it is expected that students will have been sorted into the appropriate classes and that they will be evaluated on a regular basis by a willing and able staff using the latest measures. Schools that vary from these accepted norms typically must be doing so in an effort to improve their students' performance. In fact, however, for most schools, teachers, and students, appearances are all-important. Schools, for the most part, manage the functions of guidance counselors and certified teachers, hand out textbooks, maintain buses and bus routes, attend pep rallies, assign tests and quizzes, keep records, pass bond issues, and so on. Regardless of the substance or functionality of these activities, schools continue to attend to these rituals of appropriate behavior. For many schools, so much time and effort are expended in the maintenance of appearances that there is little left for simple routine concerns, such as whether the match between students, courses, and teachers makes any educational sense. While the match between students, courses, and teachers may suit the school's need to dampen the turbulence it is attempting to control, it may make little sense for an individual student's or teacher's self-interests. Some schools seem continually buffeted by student dropouts and arrivals, changes in their administrative and teaching staff, failures of bond issues, changes in state or district graduation requirements, and attacks from irate parents and community members who question the school's legitimacy. As many school staff recognize, "if you don't put out the small fires each day, you'll get burned badly." For some schools there just never seem to be stable moments as they lurch from one dilemma to the next. Nonetheless, the school continues to sort and categorize students and teachers as successful or failed even if the original match was based on the need to solve some unrelated school problem, such as low enrollments for certain classes, a shortage of qualified teachers to teach academic courses or the students to take them, the need to generate a new curriculum to meet state requirements, or the likelihood that a large proportion of students and teachers will not be returning the following year. Whatever their problems, schools are expected to sort their students into courses with the resultant categorization of success or failure. This chapter points to the seeming capriciousness of many of the matches between students, courses, and teachers. Further it considers the implications of reform efforts, such as choice, charters, and the marketization of schooling. While providing opportunity for individual choice of schools, these reforms open up the possibility of institutionalizing collective turbulence.

　With instability and turbulence the norm for many schools, they typically find themselves in unpredictable environments. It is not uncommon that internally they struggle with turbulent student populations, aging staffs, and changing rules, roles, and responsibilities for all participants (DeLany, 1991; Lash & Kirkpatrick, 1990; Thrupp, 1995). Externalities such as changing patterns of finance, governance, and community expectations further complicate what can be a chaotic organizational environment at best. For many schools the metaphor of organized anarchies can seem more literal than figurative (March, 1994; Weick, 1976). This chapter portrays success and failure as acceptable to schools as organizations, often as the price for keeping the organization going, and often reaffirming daily routines in the lives of students, teachers, and schools. Both the categories and their implied conditions of success and failure smooth over the complications, for both schools and their participants, related to the ambiguities of preferences and identity (March, 1988; Meyer, 1987). Sorting students as failures is an imperative of schools, if only to more clearly establish the category of success. While such sorting and consequent labeling of students is in direct conflict with egalitarian ideals (Labaree, 1991), they are also essential to the retention to at least one dimension of a school's legitimacy. Schools that provide grades, tests, quizzes, class rankings, valedictorians, transcripts, and graduation diplomas have less to explain than schools that do not. In short, schools retain their legitimacy by maintaining their role as the sorting mechanism of society.

Recent efforts to "improve" schools and reduce student and school failure have shifted. This chapter briefly considers the efforts of researchers to understand how prior social policy tried to alter the mix of inputs that would raise student scores, improve dropouts, or reduce behavior problems. As a result, it catalogs the brief history of efforts to rationalize the sorting responsibility assigned to schools. Both researchers and policy analysts are seen moving closer to the "technical core," moving beyond top-down policy mandates with bottom-up strategies, and forming partnerships at the grass-roots level with teachers, students, and parents. It is generally a story of discovery by outsiders of the ambiguities and complications of teaching, learning, and running schools and classrooms. Studies of the micro-politics of schools, teaching, and learning reaffirm our understanding of schools as messy places. Efforts to stem the constant drift toward chaos in schools set the agenda and tighten the screws of what Cuban (1988) calls the "managerial imperative." The categories of success and failure become part of that effort to rationalize, sort, and dampen the messiness that threatens a school's legitimacy.

The seemingly simple and routine resource allocation decision—that of sorting teachers and students into courses—upon examination proves to be very complicated. This chapter explores these complexities as a way of understanding the micro-politics of creating success and failure. The micro-politics of who gets what courses remains untouched by the efforts of reformers to either rid a school of failure or at least rationalize it. Finally, the chapter considers the likely effects of the current shifts in social policy related to schools. Social policy efforts over the past 4 decades might be categorized as trying to improve student learning by finding the appropriate level of "inputs." Efforts at compensatory funding based on race, socioeconomic status (SES), gender, or age have met increasing attacks from critics as expensive and inefficient. It would appear that, given the inability of the inputs approach to eliminate failure and ensure success, some critics of education have begun to push for accountability, decentralization, and choice. At the same time, there is a trend for external standards and testing at the district, state, and national levels. This shift from trying to find the right mix of inputs to setting "output" standards has a recent track record in the United Kingdom, and its implications for the United States will be considered. In the United Kingdom, and elsewhere, efforts to either eliminate or rationalize failure are indicative of the ambiguities that schools, teachers, and students must work within. Like pencils, desks, and paper, students and teachers often are seen as resources to be managed, categorized, and accounted for. As the story unfolds, it will be seen that the efforts to rationalize the sorting process often are based on managing a schedule that is unrelated to the educational ends of many students. First, however, it is worthwhile to consider the micro-politics of how success and failure can be seen as a managerial concern.

THE MICRO-POLITICS OF MANAGING SUCCESS AND FAILURE

The issue of "choice" in its many forms seems firmly attached to schools, and this bond seems able to survive the fickle interests of the media, politicians, and the public. The metaphor of choice plays a prominent role in the discourse about access to particular teachers, courses, tracks, schools, grants, or local taxes. Schools provide a nexus for the intersection of beliefs about individual choice, productivity, and an optimism about the likelihood of an improved future. However, the enactment of choice in the daily routines of schools, administrators, teachers, and students requires another level of analysis. Perhaps as an extreme example of the difference between the ideal of schools and their practice, consider the following 45-second "counseling session" between an entering high school student and her "advisor" in one of this study's four schools:

COUNSELOR: You want to take geometry?
STUDENT: Not really. Is it real hard?
COUNSELOR: Yeah. Want to try it anyway? You might be able to pass.
STUDENT: I want to take classes that will get me into college.
COUNSELOR: How about advanced biology instead of reading?
STUDENT: No, I like to read.

As a result of this "counseling," a new student who had chosen foods and reading found herself placed into advanced biology and geometry. The advisor, actually the head counselor at a school where all the other counselors had been let go, had never met the student before this brief encounter. Five other students waited just outside the door for a chance to see the head of a nonexistent counseling staff, and during these first few weeks of school hundreds of students were processed with such dispatch. While the lines would die down as the first quarter progressed, there still would be a steady flow of new students transferring into this school, wanting to change classes or teachers, or in need of dropping or adding courses depending on how they were doing in their classes. In this case the counselor did not know the name of the student, much less what her background was. Her rather thin "cumulative folder" indicated reasonably good test scores and that was enough to dispense what information he could to her. A long-haired student, drumming with his drum sticks on any available surface just outside the office, reminded the counselor that he was in a rush to get back to class and he really needed to be seen. With a few more brief comments, the proper forms were finished off and the new student had been processed into her first term at this school. The student's later success or failure in geometry probably will be rationalized as her own rather than whether the match with that course, curriculum, teacher, or peers made any sense at all. Later, the results will be tabulated on grade sheets and the distinction passed down to follow her onto the next round of matches.

This particular school, dubbed School C, was one of four schools this author studied during the mid-1980s while trying to gain an understanding of how schools managed to process the curricular choices of their students. (See DeLany, 1991, and Garet & DeLany, 1988b, to further understand the messiness of the course/student match and how that seems at odds with most of the tracking literature.) What was observed at School C is not intended as an indictment of any particular school, system, or persons. With typical good cheer against insurmountable resource constraints, this school's staff worked to keep the system going. The process of scheduling students had been and remains virtually ignored. Seen as a technically neutral process, it is such a common process in the infrastructure of schools as to be invisible.

To gain some understanding of the organizational process that contributes to the curricular success or failure of students, I returned to the same schools whose transcripts had been analyzed by Garet and DeLany (1988b). For a year-and-a-half the principals, curriculum vice principals, head counselors, and math and science department chairs at the same four San Francisco Bay Area high schools allowed me to interview them and observe how they processed students into courses. Comparative case studies of how students were processed were conducted. The cases involved repeated interviews and observations of the participants, as well as observations of meetings with faculty and students. I was fortunate enough to observe the micro-politics of how courses, students, and teachers are matched in a student's daily schedule and I became convinced of how the success or failure of students is the result of multiple organizational considerations and constraints very often unrelated to a student's interests, needs, abilities, or educational goals.

The four schools differed in size, ethnic balance, average student achievement, and attrition rates. School A was an ethnically mixed, middle-class school in a relatively stable suburban neighborhood. School B was a predominantly Latino, urban, lower-middle-class school, with average achievement scores roughly 1 standard deviation below those of School A. School C was primarily a White, middle-class, suburban school; although it had the highest average reading achievement scores, it was below Schools A and D in mathematics performance. Finally, School D was a large, urban, lower-middle-class school with a substantial number of second- and third-generation Asian American students, as well as Latinos, African Americans, and recent immigrants from Southeast Asia. The four schools were representative of urban and suburban high schools, providing ethnic, achievement, and economic diversity. In their respective districts, they were not considered the best or worst examples of any teacher or student behaviors. (More specific data on the schools will be provided later.) In effect, I saw them as representative of how typical schools both construct and dole out success and failure as measured through access to their resources.

The counseling session presented above was one of many that reinforced my sense that perhaps choice in practice did not match the romantic notions of students choosing their futures through our schools (DeLany, 1991). It reiterated a theme that the overloaded school systems I was observing were able to maintain the patina of rational course choice (there were students, a counseling department, course offerings, teachers, books, etc.), but even maintaining the form left diminished resources for the school's, teachers' and students' educational substance. Consider, for example, that a highly paid senior administrator's or counselor's time and attention were consumed with merely scheduling students. Considering that the time, attention, and expertise of staff are among a school's most prized resources, the example provided from School C shows a skeletal staff moving from one client to the next to process students as quickly as possible. As the counselor said at another time, "The most important thing for success in high school is that a student start the school on the first day with the proper program." As the example points out, the notion of what is "proper" is less than obvious. One might claim that what was of primary importance to the counselor was that the student be processed/placed into classes, and the more challenging the better. But from such cursory reflections on students' behalf, the success or failure of the students in those classes will affect their family's, their teacher's, and their own assessments of their competence.

Like walking down the street and around a corner, the origins of the match take on a very different perspective and are quickly left behind as all the participants concerned try to make sense of the outcomes of a practically random assignment. Tests are given; peers, parents, school staff, and the student interpret the outcomes; and deceptive distinctions are generated based on what might be considered a capricious match of the student and the courses. To be fair, the match of student, courses, and teachers in the example above is not entirely random. The agenda of courses has been approved by the Board of Education; the student's schedule may have been signed off by her parents; the course will be taught by certified teachers; and the bureaucratic outcomes of the student's success or failure will be duly graded, made known to all, and recorded for posterity. However, the student's placement in the courses had little to do with interests, background, or competence, but rather with the need to get her into some set of courses. It is easier for the organization to justify a student with a partially arbitrary schedule of classes than one with no schedule of classes. Teachers who have no students are a greater problem than those who have too many, those who are doing badly with a reasonable number of students, or those who barely know the topic themselves. This has been noted elsewhere and typically is referred to as a decoupling of the form of schooling and its substance (Meyer & Rowan, 1977).

PRIOR EFFORTS TO UNDERSTAND SCHOOLS AS SORTERS

Contemporary discussions of school, teacher, or student failure can be considered to fall into two broad categories. Within one genre we are likely to find descriptions of schools as though they were able to "allocate" their resources differentially to diverse student populations, or students were able to "choose" their future life through the accumulation of coursework and/or human capital. Initial functionalist approaches (e.g., Parsons, 1959) assumed the proper role of schooling was to sort out students through testing, counseling, and letting "natural abilities" be provided a chance to show their capacity. With large sample surveys, Heyns (1974), Jencks and Brown (1975), Hauser, Sewell, and Alwin (1976), Alexander, Cook, and McDill (1978), and Rosenbaum (1980) broadened and refined the trail forged by the so-called Wisconsin model for educational stratification via status attainment. The assumption that schools provided course choices that were isomorphic with future life chances seemed the storyline that made sense in explaining observed outcomes. The role of schools and teachers was to act as managers of what Spring (1989) called the "sorting machine." The school's curriculum, student population, personnel, and legitimacy were considered stable and understandable, despite the distance of the surveyors, and accurate for their ability to map the steady relationship between socioeconomic status and the success or failure of students in schools.

Throughout the late 1960s, 1970s, and 1980s, another genre of research concluded that the role played by schools was not so innocent. In effect, the work of Bowles and Gintis (1976), Kerckhoff (1976), Horan (1978), McDermott and Aron (1978), Rist (1973), and later Oakes (1985) provided a storyline in which success and failure were practically allocated to students. Rather than students choosing courses, students were selected by school personnel through testing, course assignment, tracking, and noncognitive factors (such as race, gender, SES, or disruptiveness in school). Again, the sorting process schools used was characterized by coherence, intention, and consistency, as it matched types of students with types of curricula. In both the allocative and choice models there is a simple mixing of levels of effects of teachers, parents, students, and the school, as individual and organizational choices are commingled.

Successive waves of ethnographic research moved us closer to the technical core of the classroom (Mehan, 1993; Page, 1991; Rist, 1973). This research expresses concern for the powerful role teachers and counselors play in the implementation of the curriculum (Erickson & Schultz, 1982; Gamoran, 1987; Gamoran, Berends, & Nystrand, 1990; Schwille et al., 1983). It provided accounts of the influential nature of the correspondence between the students' and their families' "cultural capital" and that of school personnel (Bourdieu, 1977; Bourdieu & Passeron, 1977; Delpit, 1988; Lareau, 1989; MacLeod, 1987). Where Bourdieu helped expand beyond the economic determinism of Bowles and Gintis with concern for the relationship between social structure and the opportunity structure schools provide, there also has been the rising sense of student "choice," a reinvigoration of the agency (however misguided) that students and their families bring to the match of the school's resources and students. In a sense the analysis has come full circle from overly deterministic accounts of selection and allocation to versions of choice.

Into these changing accounts of the role schools play in stratification and individual success and failure comes the recent attention to the micro-politics of schools, led mainly by the flood of writing from the United Kingdom. Ball (1987) clearly lays out his position:

I take schools to be arenas of struggle, to be riven with actual and potential conflict between members; to be poorly co-ordinated; to be ideologically diverse. I take to be essential that if we are to understand the nature of schools as organizations, we must achieve some understanding of these conflicts. (p. 19)

While this may sound similar to Apple (1982), Boyd (1983), Giroux (1983), or others who take ideology and conflict to be the focus of their studies, the work of the UK researchers takes as its starting point a fine-grained analysis of the daily lives and work of school personnel and the community. The work typically is strewn with quotes providing the feel of life in schools from the words of participants. They portray the politics of a changing world of schooling that finds schools often submerged in a marketplace of competition with other schools (Ball, 1992; Bowe, Gewirtz, & Ball, 1994; Gewirtz, Ball, & Bowe, 1995). While the ideological and theoretical basis may not sound strikingly different, what is added is the world of teachers, students, and parents, and especially the daily work that goes on there. Much of this might be seen as an offshoot of prior work by Ball and Goodson (1985) and others related to life course changes and the ethnography of life histories. However it might be characterized, I can think of no other work as strikingly informative for the outsider since Lortie (1975) or Jackson (1968). Ball's work, like that of many of his compatriots, such as Whitty, Gewirtz, Edwards, and Bowe, stresses the centrality of power and conflict. Historically their work largely centers around the decade of Thatcherite policy changes at all levels of schooling in the United Kingdom and the corresponding financial and governance changes that supported those structural changes. Tacitly the authors describe a world consumed with the politics of its participants. The notion of politics is rather traditional in that it assumes the participants have stable preferences, are active about their interests, and tend to garner success or failure based on their access to information, power, and correspondence to dominant middle-class values.

While many of the theoretical assumptions of this work informed much of my analysis, such assumptions about stability of schooling and its participants do not seem to match my case study schools in important ways. It is not so much that the prior theories do not match schooling's impact on student success or failure, but that they fail to adequately portray how schools and their participants go about their daily lives and work while achieving those ends. Many of the recent ethnographic accounts of schooling have helped us understand the process by which success and failure are generated, but they overly prescribe orderliness and intentionality to both the participants as individuals and the school as an organization. Most certainly the recent stress inflicted by market forces on schools is unevenly distributed by students' social class affiliation. It is not necessarily that poor and working-class parents make "bad" choices for their children but that the likelihood that their children will have access to successful schools is diminished.

What is missing from the UK micro-politics work, which will be seen in several of the four U.S. case studies, is the sense of anarchy and capriciousness that occurs even after the match of students and schools has been achieved. The more successful schools and successful students are able to use their cultural capital, often through parental pressure for particular teachers and courses, to impart an orderliness to their high school careers. At the same time, individual schools look upon their pool of successful students as a resource to be exploited for the sake of the institution's legitimacy. Even within the weakest schools, the student who exhibits some academic potential will be considered a resource worth coveting. A quick dip into some of the empirical data of the case study schools will point out some of the disorder schools deal with on a regular basis and their efforts to dampen it, at least in the surface features of their daily efforts to impart the categories of success and failure to their participants.

HOW FOUR HIGH SCHOOLS MANAGED ACCESS TO COURSES

The four schools studied have much in common with each other and with normative assumptions about how schools work and process their students. Each of the four schools enrolled between 1,000 and 1,800 students; they had varying but sizable minority populations ranging from a minimum of 21% at School C to a maximum of 85% at School D; math achievement test scores varied from a maximum of the 60th percentile at School D to a minimum of the 35th percentile at School B; the reading achievement test scores varied from a maximum of the 57th percentile at School C to a minimum of the 31st percentile at School B; attrition rates varied, with only 35% of the entering class at School B still enrolled by their senior year, while at School C 63% of the students who entered in the ninth grade were enrolled as twelfth graders at the school. As in other studies, it was found that achievement test scores were significantly related to initial course placement and student success or failure. In their own way, all the schools were appropriately interested in the most recent curriculum, testing, and research. All the schools had counseling departments and voluminous information on students and their prior performance; all the schools had parent–teacher associations and alumni/ae; and all the schools had similar procedures by which they scheduled their students and teachers into courses.

What Students Actually Took

A closer look at what students actually took yields some surprising results both within particular schools and across the schools. Summarizing some of the results that stand out, a number of findings are worth mentioning. First, the routes students took through the curriculum varied from school to school and subject to subject. For example, at School A students followed more than 60 distinct paths through the science curriculum, while the route considered the *norm* (biology, chemistry, physics) was followed by only 7% of the students. Within the science program the most likely pattern was the biology class in the tenth grade followed by no further science; still, that route was taken by only 16% of the students; 15% took the life science class followed by no further science. Each of the other schools had similar variations from the expected norm.

Second, while achievement test scores were significant predictors of student course placement, they were fairly imperfect. For example, at three of the four schools, students at the 25th percentile in math achievement had some chance of taking algebra in tenth grade, and students at the 75th percentile were far from certain of taking tenth-grade geometry.

Third, there are substantial differences in course placement probabilities across the four schools. For example, when controlling for ethnicity, gender, test scores, and a student's school, a student at the 50th percentile in math achievement had a 16% chance of taking algebra or geometry in the tenth grade at School A, a 72% chance at School B, a 46% chance at School C, and a 27% chance at School D. The probability of taking no mathematics at all ranged from 19% at School B to 70% at School D. In science, taking either biology or general science in tenth grade for students at the 50th percentile had equally large variations, 95% at School A, 83% at School B, 47% at School C, and 68% at School D. The probability of taking no science ranged from 5% at School A to 53% at School C.

Fourth, the pattern of association across disciplines was not as regular as typically is presumed. The assumption that students in tenth grade would be taking geometry and biology seemed not to hold: At both School A and School B only 9% were taking those courses their sophomore year, while at School C 19% and at School D 33% were enrolled in those courses. It was found that students taking algebra in tenth grade were taking all levels in the science curriculum, and students taking biology could be found at all levels of math. As a result, the assumptions about the ubiquity of tracking did not seem to hold as might be expected. Students did not necessarily take only top math, science, and English classes, but seemed to take courses at varying levels across the disciplines.

Student and Teacher Turbulence

In addition to the diverse and unexpected routes students took through the curriculum, it is worth describing the demographics of student, teacher, and curricular turbulence. It typically is assumed that these three aspects of a school are stable. For example, when a study reports that there are $X\%$ of students or teachers with Y characteristics, what is missing is that while the percentages may remain stable throughout the year, the individual students, teachers, or courses actually may be different. The stable percentages provide the illusion of stability, which many schools lack when viewed from the ground level and on a daily basis. There were several indications of the variability of turbulence at the four case study schools.

First, each school's teaching staff changed from year to year but at different rates. For example, while Schools A, C, and D had around 12% turnover, School B had 21% turnover. That means that at School B more than one-fifth of the teachers were new to the school and its curriculum expectations, were unknown by the students and other staff, and were scheduled to teach classes of students for whom they had no prior expectations. Curricular planning by the school's administration was complicated by not knowing whether the new faculty members would be capable of teaching the curriculum, since the hiring was done at the district rather than the school level.

Second, each school's student population changed both during the year and over the summer. While accurate counts of the school-year turnover were not available, the changes over the summer were startling. While Schools A, C, and D had between 10% and 14% student turnover, School B had more than 25% turnover. Turnover numbers often can be confusing since there is seldom a sense of when the changes occur. If in addition to the changes that occurred over the summer, we were to consider what occurred during the school year, the net change in the student population would be even greater. To be more specific, Schools D and B provided the sharpest contrasts. At School D, 11% (339 students) of the students for whom course and teacher schedules were prepared in the previous spring did not show up in the fall. Adding to that confusion at School D, an additional 10% (307) of the student body arrived needing to be scheduled. At School B, 27% (311) of those scheduled during the previous spring term did not show up, and an additional 25% (268) arrived who needed to be quickly scheduled into classes with teachers (a fifth of whom were new to the school).

Third, with reforms in the state's high school graduation requirements in full swing in the late 1980s, 2 years of math and 2 years of science were

required as well as a "fine arts" course or a year of language. The requirements were phased in so that they were different for each year's cohort.
What actually constituted these courses was not clear according to school
personnel but required negotiations with the state. State and local mandates
concerning increased graduation requirements seldom included additional
staff resources. Additions to the curriculum from the spring to the fall of 1986,
in terms of changes in course titles offered, ranged from 4% to 63%, with the
vast majority of changes coming in what were considered nonacademic areas
(Agnew, 1987).

Fourth, for symbolic and political reasons, advanced courses were kept
open despite low enrollments, increasing the student/teacher ratio in lower-
level courses. All four schools did their best, with varying success, to de-
ceive their district offices about the enrollments in their advanced courses.
District offices were less sensitive to the needs of faculty and students to
maintain low-enrollment, yet academically high-status, courses since low-
enrollment courses cost more in terms of student/teacher ratios. One of the
few advantages that School B possessed was that because of its steady turnover of students and teachers, the district was less able to challenge its accounting of how many students it had or teachers it needed. The turbulence,
in this case, became an organizational advantage for acquiring resources.

As might be expected, many of these demographic shifts in the student and teacher population, when combined with the changing curricular requirements, produced what has been called in other situations an
"organized anarchy." This is not to say that students, teachers, and courses
were not in place in the fall of each year. School staff worked far beyond
their union standards to get each school's schedule in order. That entailed
evenings and weekends as the opening of school approached. Arguments
with the district about enrollment projections and subsequent teaching staff
needs heightened as the first day approached. As might be expected, there
were variations across the case study schools in the resources available to
handle such turbulence. In addition, as has been noted elsewhere (Choy &
Gifford, 1980), there were variations in how each of the schools was supported by its district office.

Master Schedules and the Appearance of Order

A school's master schedule sits as the matrix into which is poured the
daily agenda of every student and teacher. Its orderly offerings of time,
classes, teachers, and students masks the political infighting that contributed to its construction. Negotiations with the district, union, state, parents, teachers, and students continue throughout the school year. None-

theless, it is the beginning of each school year that is particularly telling about the intentionality of the match of students, teachers, and courses. In addition to the political nature of the matching process, it certainly looms as a formidable information processing problem that few schools are adequately equipped to handle either in the initial stages of constructing the master schedule or in the later stages of attempting to monitor student progress and allow that information to inform either student, teacher, or school level decisions.

Seen as an information processing problem, the work of the school personnel takes on a further poignant aspect. As mentioned earlier, all the schools had counseling departments. However, only Schools A and D still had more than a single person who might be called a "counselor." Schools B and C had an individual doing all the assigning of students to teachers' classes. The counseling session presented at the beginning of the chapter involved the head of counseling and the sole remaining member of the counseling staff, the rest having been "pink slipped" during the early 1980s. School C's counselor kept his system going by creating "Clerk" as a possible course that students could take for credit. Students received credit toward graduation, while the school avoided having to pay secretarial salaries and benefits. With 105 student clerks and 62 technical clerks, School C was able to keep up with monitoring student progress and the general surveillance of student records.

While Schools A and D had full complements of full-time counselors, there were still opportunities for confusion. School A's yearly arguments with district administrators focused on projected student enrollments. The school would claim that it needed additional teachers because it anticipated more incoming students than the district planners did. The number of students attending any school can be translated directly into state financial support when course enrollment caps are taken into account. The schools want additional teachers to meet their needs, and the district tries to reduce costs by hiring only the minimum number of teachers needed. During the opening of school in 1983, School D found itself short seven teachers. It was months before students were sorted into newly created sections of overenrolled courses and courses taught by substitute teachers. During this time the excess students met in the gym and other available spaces. The notion of administrative turmoil also comes into play here. Two years later when there was turnover in administrators at School D, the incoming assistant principal in charge of scheduling students discovered on reporting the week before the opening of school that the departing person in charge of that work had not finished the master schedule. More than 100 students had no schedule and another 600 still had conflicts that had not been resolved. The departing scheduler had decided to focus on her new school, while the incoming scheduler had worked to complete the schedule for the school he was leaving. During the transition, the maintenance of School D's schedule had been forgotten.

A similar administrative shift at School A produced an equally chaotic beginning to the school year. The previous principal, who had always done the scheduling himself, had left on a year's sabbatical. While the schedule had been completed in the summer, the novice administrator now in charge of scheduling found that district efforts to improve the computer programming of the school's scheduling system were faulty. Each time the system generated schedules for new students, it altered the schedules of all the other students. In addition to mixing up the master schedule for the coming year, it incorrectly generated transcripts of recent graduates. This was the same system that the previous, experienced principal knew was defective but saw as useful in that it produced inflated numbers of students enrolled for the next year.

Faulty information systems were not uncommon in the case study schools. Typically, it was understood that the systems were not necessarily purchased for the scheduling of students, but rather for such district uses as payroll, record keeping, and other personnel needs. Although School B faced technical problems similar to those at School A in that its system seemed incapable of producing student rankings and transcripts, its main problem was having no counselors and only a single administrator to generate and maintain the schedule. School B is a classic case of a resource-poor organization trying to maintain order and keep the system working in expected ways. During a typical hour in his office near the end of the day, the administrator/counselor/scheduler of School B saw 18 people an hour. The changes were as diverse and complicated as at the other schools, but at the end of the day there was the announcement that all students needing changes were to report to the auditorium. A remarkable number and diversity of students (African Americans, Latinos, and Portuguese, Vietnamese, Samoan, and Tongan Americans, among others) good-naturedly took their numbered slips of paper as they filed into the auditorium. The scheduler, sitting behind a long table, called out the numbers and students' grievances were heard, cumulative folders consulted, and schedules changed. With all the efficiency of a deli, and with the help of two aides, students were "counseled" through course and teacher changes at rate of more than five students a minute. Although he had only half an hour available, the counselor/administrator was able to work through 128 students before announcing to the remaining crowd that they could come back the next day if they still needed a change. School B had the highest student (26%) and teacher (21%) turnover of all the schools. Within the first month, 242 students arrived and 186 left.

The Frog Pond Dilemma

There was certainly wide variation across the schools in the extent to which they could "rationally" sort their students according to normative assumptions about the value of testing, counseling, and parental involvement. There is an ironic twist to what might be considered the "outcomes" of the sorting process: School B provided the greatest probability for minority students to gain access to academic coursework. School B might just stand out as an unexpected "frog pond" (DeLany, 1993; Meyer, 1970; Thrupp, 1995). The old problem of whether one would want to be a big frog in a small pond or a small frog in a big pond comes into play here. Minority students of comparable academic achievement were more likely to be taking academic coursework at School B than comparable students in the other three schools. Being in the "bigger pond" of School A, C, or D would have lowered the chances of comparable minority students gaining access to academic classes. Although it had a high proportion of minority students (84% overall with 70% Latino) with low achievement test scores (thirty-first percentile in reading and thirty-fifth percentile in math), and in a sense was considered a "small pond," School B offered improved probabilities of access to an academic curriculum over the other schools (Garet & DeLany, 1988a).

Questions concerning the effect of the distribution of student ability and/or socioeconomic status in a school are not new and currently are centered on what is called "school mix." School mix, as a theoretical construct, has re-emerged as a school variable with implications for learning and access to the curriculum. The work of Coleman and colleagues (1966) and Jencks et al. (1972) downplayed school effects on student outcomes over and above the influence of student background characteristics. The literature (as well as a version of common sense) indicates that schools and classrooms with large numbers of low-ability students are constrained in ways that more favorably composed schools are not (Barr & Dreeben, 1983). The general notion of the effect of students as a resource in a school has been that the composition of their abilities influences the "ethos" for effectiveness in schools (Rutter, Maughan, Mortimore, & Ouston, 1979). More systematic work by Sorensen (1987) and Sorensen and Hallinan (1986), discussing the academic careers of students, points out that access to academic coursework depends on the availability of slots in academic courses, regardless of the distribution of ability. As a result, the notion of upward mobility in the chain of increasingly more advanced coursework, can be seen to depend on the "pond" in which a student happens to be floating. Access to opportunities for success or failure is dependent not strictly on individual student traits but on the mix of traits in a school and how the organization values those traits.

INTERPRETING THE MICRO-POLITICS
OF SCHOOLS AS ORGANIZATIONS

Organizationally it is useful for schools in need of managing their unstable environments to decouple the scheduling process from assumptions about the efficacy of the *choices* or course *selections* provided to students. Access to opportunities for success or failure can be managed like any other resource, while presenting to the outside world the appearance of a legitimate, rationally organized matching of students, teachers, and courses. It should be evident that the decoupling of the actual work of scheduling from the forms, timelines, parental permission slips, locator cards, and all the other trappings of the process results in part from there being no shared, well-defined technology for knowing which students should be taking which courses. While there might be social norms for the matching of students and courses, there is an absence of much of the knowledge that would facilitate matching students with courses appropriate to their needs. It is classified most easily as a craft rather than a science. As a craft, it requires time, attention, and an intimate knowledge of the students, teachers, parents, and community. Such craft knowledge as might have been used to facilitate individual matches was superseded by the craft of facilitating organizational needs.

For many school administrators, it is imperative that they dampen the uncertainty and disorder of their schools, meet deadlines and expectations, and manage the time, tools, and people for whom they are responsible. As Cuban (1988) points out, the managerial imperative takes over in many situations and overrides individual educational wants or needs. This issue has arisen in studies of student mobility in such decentralized systems as Chicago's (Kerbow, 1993). Chicago students choose their schools, and with that freedom comes the inability of schools to predict how many students will be enrolling from year to year. Especially under conditions of resource shortage (where the notion of resources is expanded to include successful students, time, and legitimacy), schools act in ways that so many other organizations do. Schools begin to dispense failure and success for their students, at times, as secondary outcomes to their daily work of controlling their turbulence. As a result, access to particular curricula and teachers, often seemingly irrational, is interpreted by the participants as indicative of students' individual success or failure. Even in benign cases where schools try their best in turbulent circumstances, the results can be the same. The match of students and courses can satisfy a different logic. A managerial imperative relegates students' best interests to a secondary role. At the same time, we saw that School B, the most turbulent of the four schools, provided minority students with the best chance for access to an academic curriculum.

The preceding sections of this chapter described how the case study schools process students toward courses, tracks, and teachers. The descriptions portray the emphasis on the sorting process, its regularity, surface rationality (in organizational rather than individual student or teacher terms), and the micro-politics of who gets what in terms of the teachers, students, and course offerings. As other writers (e.g., Elmore, 1991) have mentioned, "regularity" is of great importance to schools. While all of this is helpful in our understanding of the motives that generate schoolwork and the arbitrary nature of the consequent labels and environments from which both student success and student failure follow, I feel that it over-rates the regularities of daily school life. Prior descriptions of the micro-politics of schools impart far too much rationality to the processes they use. As demonstrated, the variation across schools indicates that students have better or worse chances of access to academic coursework. Despite all the trappings of rationality that the schools expended on their sorting, there was little attention to the decision about what courses students would take. Beyond rules of thumb derived to hasten the process of getting students into classes, not much organizational attention was expended on who might best benefit except in organizational terms. Even at School B, where minority students had the highest probability of access to an academic curriculum, concerns about maintenance of the school's legitimacy led it to "dip down" into the student pool of the lower achievement levels to keep up enrollments in its academic courses. Most of the schools were willing to minimize the resource drain that the sorting process might extract. At the same time, all attempted to extract from their districts as much as they could based on inflated enrollment projections and numbers.

Whether the student outcomes are or would be any different is problematic, but it is worthwhile critiquing the theoretical models that view power, position, and intention as so formative of the outcomes. In the counseling session presented earlier, the counselor followed his rule of thumb that the most important item in student placement was speed. The caveat that the student's course placement also should be "appropriate" was lost in the rush of the "street-level bureaucrats" to meet the daily obligations and commitments negotiated by the school's administrators with the school's environment (Weatherly & Lipskey, 1977). That environment includes the state, the district, the local community, the teachers' unions, individual teachers, and students and parents, all of whom hover about the school's resources.

This is not to say that all parents, students, teachers, or administrators had equal access to the decisions that the schedule embodies. Instead, it makes sense to see the construction of the schedule as the result of the confluence of three streams: participants, solutions, and problems. The participants are the parents, students, faculty, district, community, and state. The solutions are the curriculum, the schedule, teachers' credentials, classrooms, and textbooks. The problems vary according to participant. For students, there are questions like, "What courses should I take?" or "What courses will my friends be in?" School administrators worry about what courses to offer and which teachers should be teaching them with which books. Taxpayers are concerned with reducing the cost of schooling and how much money they want to spend on the schools; with who can be a teacher and how to tell if they are good enough; with how and what should be taught, and so forth. As the case studies suggest, the participants come and go with the turbulence of teachers, administrators, students, and their families, as do the curriculum and graduation requirements. In School B a proportion of the population came and went, barely touching down in the community for more than a few days, months, or a year. At School C the influx of an unstable student group and the departure of the counseling staff left a dislocation between many of the students and staff. In both schools the "stable" students and parents became a resource to be hoarded and attended to. The likelihood of success with and for students and the expenditure of school resources needed to support that success were easily seen to rest with the student groups that reliably returned each year and provided a bulwark for the schools in an otherwise disorderly environment. The problems to be solved vary both in content and intensity, and range from dropouts, school choice, teen pregnancy, religion in the curriculum, teacher competency (or teacher autonomy), community disinterest (or trying to keep politics out of schools), rigorous curriculum (or reader-appropriate curriculum), or schools that cost too much (or are financially neglected). The constant battles with "downtown" or "central administration" led all the case study schools to manipulate student enrollment counts. Lowered estimates of the number of students meant lowered estimates of the number of full-time equivalent teachers made available to the schools. School A was able to use faulty computer programming during the scheduling process to bulk up its numbers; School B double-counted students by including those it knew or believed would not return. Schools C and D had increasing difficulty padding their enrollments. While trying to make their schools more manageable, their managers lived by the dictum that no information is "innocent" (March, 1994).

Of central theoretical importance to interpreting the case study schools is the notion that a "temporal sorting" model often seems more applicable than a "consequential sorting" model for understanding the role schools play in sorting students and teachers toward success or failure. Events are "temporally" related because they occur at the same time rather than because there is a causal relation between them or one is the consequence of the other. Researchers have identified the effects of temporal sorting in various settings, including military engagements (Metcalf, 1986), legislative agenda setting (Kingdon, 1984), accident prevention (Perrow, 1984), school desegregation efforts (Weiner, 1976), high school scheduling (DeLany, 1991) and accounting (Cooper, Hayes, & Wolf, 1981). All of these situations are described as "organized anarchies." In the sorting of students, courses, and teachers there are unclear preferences, and success is often ambiguous. The available technology provides no clear rules for producing success or failure beyond the mere existence of the completed schedule. The participation in decisions is fluid, with steady turnover in decision makers (students, parents, teachers, and administrators all trying to exert influence over the final schedule) and places where decisions get made (the prior fall's opportunity for students to choose their next year's courses, students' homes, administrative planning sessions, or School B's packed auditorium). For some schools, like School B, temporal sorting seems the norm.

Many theorists argue that opportunities for success or failure are allocated, chosen, or negotiated by critical participants (such as teachers, schedulers, counselors, and parents) through their attention, efforts, and belief in the primacy of consequential actions. For many participants, there is a sense of strategic and consequential order to their choices of schools, courses, teachers, and tracks. At the same time, their actions reveal an ambivalence. Thus teachers value test results, yet they also realize that the tests are culturally insensitive and typically unrelated to what is taught in classes. Parents and students show intense concern for grade reports, yet they also know that grades are largely affected by teacher and peer perceptions of noncognitive student traits. Schedulers and counselors spend much of their time and attention gathering data on students' prior achievement, ability, and interests, even though when course decisions are made, the data are often not available, either because there is no time to consult them or because they are inaccessible or in an unusable form. Finally, parents and their children try to choose appropriate course trajectories, even though their sense of alternatives is constrained by their own cultural capital. As a result, I would argue, rather than choices being strategically based on assumptions of consequences, student, teacher, and course matches often come down to what is available at the time. And availability is an institutional rather than an individual consideration.

CONCLUSION

As Weick (1978) notes, it is essential to spend more time watching leaders "on line" in the belief that "some of the least important realities about leaders are being accorded some of the largest [amounts of] attention" (p. 60). As he points out:

We have to put ourselves in a better position to watch leaders make do, let it pass, improvise, make inferences, scramble, and all the other things that leaders do during their days between more visible moments of glory. (p. 60)

The case study schools portray school leaders scrambling to keep their schools on track and contending with the likelihood of impending or actual anarchy that surrounds them. The descriptions of how they match up students, courses, and teachers provide examples of improvisation, cutting corners, and coping on a daily basis. While their efforts often make organizational sense, the choices they make for students and teachers often make little individual sense. For successful students, the match of student, teacher, and course can be seen as the result of consequential decisions. Other students and teachers can find themselves in courses because the placement serves the needs of the school. At times teachers find themselves "shoehorned," as one administrator put it, into classes because no one else is available to teach them. Students can find themselves in classes because nothing else was open or the administration needed to increase enrollments in a course. These examples of what was referred to as temporal sorting typically happen under times of managerial stress, shortages of time and attention, and the need to get on with the next task. For students with low resource value to a school, the opportunities for access to successful curricular opportunities are limited by such haphazard improvisations as serve the school's managerial needs.

Teachers also become labeled as "successes" or "failures" in many of the same ways their students do. The sorting of teachers into lower- and higher-track courses becomes difficult to overcome. Teachers who find themselves relegated to lower-track classes often begin to feel the same lowered sense of self-efficacy their students do. Many teachers are unwilling to teach general math, general science, remedial reading, or other courses associated with unsuccessful students. Department chairs are often unwilling to upset their successful teachers who are already doing a credible job with higher-track classes. Meanwhile, administrators are unwilling to concoct dubious explanations to the parents of successful students as to why their best teachers might not be available because of shifts to lower-track courses. Once typecast as a teacher of lower-track classes, it is often difficult to shed that label. In addition, teachers of lower-track classes begin to experience all the disadvantages this chapter has outlined. Resources such as time, attention, books, chairs, and chalk often become in short supply for courses, teachers, and students that are not considered of either symbolic or functional value to the school's management. In addition, the likelihood of success with remedial classes is low since the students, for the most part, are more likely to be absent, less motivated, less academically able, and more disruptive. Finally, teachers labeled as failures are less likely to be consulted by the community, the administration, their fellow faculty members, or students for their perceptions about how to improve the school. "Failed" teachers, unlike "failed" students, do not always drop out of school. Instead, they can continue for years in their position of tending "failed" students in what might be considered a means for "cutting one's losses."

How might one of the more prominent reform efforts affect such matches of students, courses, and teachers and their likelihood of access to opportunities? Efforts in other countries to generate a "marketplace" for schools, centralized testing, parental school choice, and site-based budgeting and management provide hints at the possibilities for U.S. schools (Whitty, 1996). If anything, they would indicate that there is a great deal to worry about for poorer students and teachers. The examples given of matching students, teachers, and courses can be expanded beyond the individual school to entire locales. Students who are seen as potential resources for schools trying to improve their scores on centralized tests and who impose few "costs" on a school truly will have choices of where they would like to attend. Schools that are undersubscribed will acquire students rejected by the more successful schools. Rather than choosing their schools, courses, and teachers, many students will find their access to educational opportunities the result of temporal sorting. The marketplace will determine what is left over for them. One might anticipate clear changes in the distribution of success and failure between schools, as successful students are allowed into successful schools. The rest will be left to fend for themselves as best they can. Further, if attention was already in short supply for some schools, the marketplace will further deplete that valuable resource. Heightened demands for "public relations," a curriculum that will improve centralized test scores, drastically increased budgetary concerns, and the need to recruit the best students will be added to an administrator's job description.

These four case studies do not provide an overly romantic version of how student access to opportunity is managed currently. Seen as organizations managing their resources and dampening disorder, the schools did well. At the individual level, though, students and teachers often were matched with courses that made little educational sense. While the micro-politics of that allocation of curricular resources is fascinating to the outsider, that storyline is less than consoling to the students and teachers who found themselves in classes that were simply of institutional convenience. I would concur with others (Elmore & Fuller, 1996; Wells, 1993) that the introduction of markets is likely to increase social segregation and inequalities in our pluralistic society. Our concern for the nonmarket failures of education may soon shift to the dangers of the market failure of schools.

The hidden hand of the marketplace will do little to improve the efforts of school managers to equitably provide educational opportunity for all their students.

REFERENCES

Agnew, J. (1987). *High schools and shopping malls.* Unpublished doctoral dissertation, Stanford University, Stanford.

Alexander, K. L., Cook, M., & McDill, E. (1978). Curriculum tracking and educational stratification: Some further evidence. *American Sociological Review, 43,* 47–66.

Apple, M. (1982). *Education and power.* Boston: Routledge & Kegan Paul.

Ball, S. (1987). *The micro-politics of the school.* New York: Methuen.

Ball, S. (1992, April). Schooling, enterprise and the market. In *The globalization of a reform strategy: the role of the market in school reform.* Symposium conducted at the annual meeting of the American Educational Research Association. San Francisco.

Ball, S., & Goodson, I. (1985). *Teachers' lives and careers.* London: Falmer Press.

Barr, R., & Dreeben, R. (1983). *How schools work.* Chicago: University of Chicago Press.

Bourdieu, P. (1977). Cultural reproduction and social reproduction. In J. Karabel & A. Halsey (Eds.), *Power and ideology in education* (pp. 487–511) New York: Oxford University Press.

Bourdieu, P., & Passeron, C. (1977). *Reproduction in education, society, and culture.* London: Sage.

Bowe, R., Gewirtz, S., & Ball, S. (1994). Captured by the discourse? Issues and concerns in researching "parental choice." *British Journal of Sociology of Education, 15*(1), 63–78.

Bowles, S., & Gintis, H. (1976). *Schooling in capitalist America.* New York: Basic Books.

Boyd, W. (1983, November). Rethinking educational policy and management: Political science and educational administration in the 1980s. *American Journal of Education,* pp. 1–29.

Choy, R., & Gifford, B. (1980, Summer). Resource allocation in a segregated school system: The case of Los Angeles. *Journal of Educational Finance,* pp. 34–50.

Coleman, J., Campbell, E., Hobson, C., McPartland, J., Mood, A., Weinfeld, F., & York, R. (1966). *Equality of educational opportunity.* Washington, DC: U.S. Government Printing Office.

Cooper, D., Hayes, D., & Wolf, F. (1981). Accounting in organized anarchies: Understanding and designing accounting systems in ambiguous situations. *Accounting, Organizations, and Society, 6,* 175–191.

Cuban, L. (1988). *The managerial imperative and the practice of leadership in schools.* Albany: State University of New York Press.

Delpit, L. (1988). The silenced dialogue: Power and pedagogy in educating other people's children. *Harvard Education Review, 58,* 280–298.

DeLany, B. (1991). Allocation, choice, and stratification within high schools: How the sorting machine copes. *American Journal of Education, 99*, 181–207.

DeLany, B. (1993, April). *The frog pond revisited: The management of students as resources.* Paper presented at the annual meeting of the American Educational Research Association, Atlanta.

Elmore, R. (1991, April). Teaching, learning, and organization: School restructuring and recurring dilemmas of reform. Paper presented at the annual meeting of the American Educational Research Association, Chicago.

Elmore, R., & Fuller, B. (1996). *Who chooses? Who loses?* New York: Teachers College Press.

Erickson, F., & Schultz, J. (1982). *The counselor as gatekeeper: Social interaction in interviews.* New York: Academic Press.

Gamoran, A. (1987). The stratification of high school learning opportunities. *Sociology of Education, 60*, 135–155.

Gamoran, A., Berends, M., & Nystrand, M. (1990, April). *Classroom instruction and the effects of ability grouping: A structural model.* Paper presented at the annual meeting of the American Educational Research Association, Boston.

Garet, M., & DeLany, B. (1988a, April). *Course sequences as organizational careers: Models of curriculum mobility in high school math and science.* Paper presented at the annual meeting of the American Educational Research Association, New Orleans.

Garet, M., & DeLany, B. (1988b). Students, courses, and stratification. *Sociology of Education, 61*, 661–677.

Gewirtz, S., Ball, S., & Bowe, R. (1995). *Markets, choice, and equity in education.* Buckingham: Open University Press.

Giroux, H. (1983). *Theory of resistance.* South Hadley, MA: Bergin & Garvey.

Hauser, R. M., Sewell, W., & Alwin, D. (1976). High school effects on achievement. In W. Sewell, R. M. Hauser, & D. Featherman (Eds.), *Schooling and achievement in American society* (pp. 309–341). New York: Academic Press.

Heyns, B. (1974). Social selection and stratification within schools. *American Journal of Sociology, 79*, 1434–1451.

Horan, P. (1978). Is status attainment research atheoretical? *American Sociological Review, 43*, 534–541.

Jackson, P. (1968). *Life in classrooms.* New York: Holt, Rinehart and Winston.

Jencks, C., & Brown, M. (1975). Effects of high schools on their students. *Harvard Educational Review, 46*, 273–324.

Jencks, C., Smith, M., Ackland, H., Bane, M. J., Cohen, D., Gintis, H., Heyns, B., & Michelson, S. (1972). *Inequality.* New York: Basic Books.

Kerbow, D. (1993, April). *Instructional practice and student mobility: Networks of student exchange in inner-city schools.* Paper presented at the annual meeting of the American Educational Research Association, Atlanta.

Kerckhoff, A. C. (1976). The status attainment process: Socialization or allocation? *Social Forces, 55*, 368–381.

Kingdon, J. (1984). *Agendas, alternatives, and public policies.* Boston: Little, Brown.

Labaree, D. (1991, October). *An unlovely legacy: The disabling impact of the market on American teacher education.* A plenary address presented at the Conference on Continuity and Change in Teacher Education, University of Western Ontario, London, Ontario.

Lareau, A. (1989). *Home advantage: Social class and parental intervention in elementary education.* Philadelphia: Falmer Press.

Lash, A., & Kirkpatrick, S. (1990). A classroom perspective of student mobility. *Elementary School Journal, 91*, 177–191.

Lortie, D. (1975). *Schoolteacher: A sociological study.* Chicago: University of Chicago Press.

MacLeod, J. (1987). *Ain't no makin' it: Leveled aspirations in a low-income neighborhood.* Boulder, CO: Westview.

March, J. G. (1988). A chronicle of speculations about organizational decision-making. In J. G. March (Ed.), *Decisions and organizations* (pp. 1–21). Oxford: Blackwell.

March, J. G. (1994). *A primer on decision making.* New York: Free Press.

McDermott, R., & Aron, J. (1978). Pirandello in the classroom: On the possibility of equal educational opportunity in American culture. In M. Reynolds (Ed.), *Futures of education for exceptional children: Emerging structures* (pp. 41–64). London: National Support System Project.

Mehan, H. (1993). Understanding inequality in schools: The contribution of interpretive studies. *Sociology of Education, 65*, 1–20.

Metcalf, J. (1986). Decision making and the Granada rescue operation. In J. G. March & R. Weissinger-Baylon (Eds.), *Ambiguity and command: Organizational perspectives on military decision making* (pp. 227–296). New York: Longman.

Meyer, J. (1970). High school effects on college intentions. *American Journal of Sociology, 76*, 59–70.

Meyer, J. (1987). Self and life course: Institutionalization and its effects. In G. Thomas, J. Meyer, F. Ramirez, & J. Boli (Eds.), *Institutional structure: Constituting state, society, and the individual* (pp. 242–260). Beverly Hills: Sage.

Meyer, J., & Rowan, B. (1977, September). Institutionalized organizations: Formal structure as myth and ceremony. *American Journal of Sociology, 83*, 440–463.

Oakes, J. (1985). *Keeping track: How schools structure inequality.* New Haven: Yale University Press.

Page, R. (1991). *Lower-track classrooms: A curricular and cultural perspective.* New York: Teachers College Press.

Parsons, T. (1959). The school as a social system: Some of its functions in American society. *Harvard Educational Review, 29*(4), 292–318.

Perrow, C. (1984). *Normal accidents: Living with high risk technologies.* New York: Basic Books.

Rist, R. (1973). *The urban school: A factory for failure.* Cambridge, MA: MIT Press.

Rosenbaum, J. (1980). Track misperception and frustrated college plans: An analysis of the effects of track and track perceptions in the NLS. *Sociology of Education, 53*, 74–88.

Rutter, M., Maughan, B., Mortimore, P., & Ouston, J. (1979). *Fifteen thousand hours.* Cambridge, MA: Harvard University Press.

Schwille, J., Porter, A., Belli, G., Floden, R., Freeman, D., Knappen, L., Kuhs, T., & Schmidt, W. (1983) . Teachers as policy brokers in the content of elementary school mathematics. In L. S. Schulman & G. Sykes (Eds.), *Handbook of teaching and policy* (pp. 370–391). New York: Longman.

Sorensen, A. (1987). The organizational differentiation of students in school as an opportunity structure. In M. Hallinan (Ed.), *The social organization of schools: New conceptualizations of the learning process* (pp. 103–129). New York: Plenum.

Sorensen, A., & Hallinan, M. (1986). Effects of ability grouping on growth in academic achievement. *American Educational Research Journal, 23,* 519–542.

Spring, J. (1989). *The sorting machine revisited: National educational policy since 1945.* White Plains, NY: Longman.

Thrupp, M. (1995). The school mix effect: The history of an enduring problem in educational research, policy and practice. *British Journal of Sociology of Education, 16*(2), 183–203.

Weatherly, R., & Lipskey, M. (1977). Street-level bureaucrats and institutional innovation: Implementing special-education reform. *Harvard Educational Review, 47*(2), 171–197.

Weick, K. (1976). Educational organizations as loosely coupled systems. *Administrative Science Quarterly, 21,* 1–19.

Weick, K. (1978). The spines of leaders. In M. W. McCall, Jr. & M. Lombardo (Eds.), *Leadership: Where else can we go?* (pp. 41–74). Durham, NC: Duke University Press.

Weiner, S. (1976). Participation, deadlines, and choice. In J. G. March & J. Olsen (Eds.), *Ambiguity and choice in organizations* (pp. 225–250). Bergen, Norway: Universitetsforlaget.

Wells, A. S. (1993). *Time to choose: America at the crossroads of school choice policy.* New York: Hill & Wang.

Whitty, G. (1996). Creating quasi-markets in education: A review of recent research on parental choice and school autonomy in three countries. *Review of Research in Education, 22,* 1–83.

CHAPTER 8

Some Musings on What Can Be Done

HENRY M. LEVIN

The chapters in this volume focus on the failure of two closely connected groups, students and teachers. Presumably, when students fail, it is at least partially a reflection on the efforts, skills, and professionalism of their teachers. This leads to teacher frustration, sadness, anger, self-doubt, and loss of esteem. Some teachers respond with heroic efforts to decrease student failure, but with only mixed results. They constantly search for "break-throughs" and try many things, with only partial success. Others accept student failure as inevitable because of the unstable family and economic situations of their students, inadequate school resources such as large class sizes, and limited interest and ability on the part of some students. They view themselves as doing the best that they can in the circumstances, a theme that echoes throughout Daniel Lortie's (1975) classic on how teachers view their own work. Nevertheless, they still feel blamed for factors beyond their control.

The focus of this chapter is to reflect on what might be done to reduce both student and teacher failure. I have deliberately referred to this excursion as "musings" in order to warn the reader that I am providing some thoughts on the subject rather than a comprehensive understanding and solution. The obvious reasons for caution are that both the definitions and perceptions of failure and their causes go well beyond what normally is thought of as the purview of educational policy. Thus, we might be able to identify some of the obstacles to change, but not the strategies to surmount them.

It should be noted at the outset that I will advocate a radical restructuring of the schooling experience to reduce both teacher and student fail-

ure on the basis that failure is an inevitable product of the present schooling approach. That is, I lay much of the cause of failure at the door of the
existing way in which schools are constituted. However, I want to stress at
this point that nothing in this chapter provides a good excuse for lacklus-
ter effort and the "boring repetition of subject matter" approach that students have criticized in the chapter by Richard Altenbaugh.

WHAT IS MEANT BY FAILURE?

A major challenge in addressing both student failure and its impact on teachers is the ambiguity surrounding both what student and teacher failure
means and its causes. Student failure is a socially constructed term (see the
chapter by Lynda Stone for a discussion). One cannot have failure without
understanding and expectations of what success means. Students, parents,
and teachers all have a general picture of what success or failure means to
them, a picture heavily conditioned on the messages of school authorities,
peers, and the media. Of course, when individuals apply this to their own
situations, the details may differ according to their personal experiences. To
a highly aspiring parent or student, school success may mean nothing less
than straight As. To a less aspiring parent or student, it may mean passing
courses and graduating. But, even these expectations derive from prior experiences, such as previous levels of accomplishment, as well as the embedded expectations among members of their communities.

At a societal level, we probably have a clearer picture of what constitutes school success or failure because of the institutional framework that
is imposed. Failure refers to the failure of students to meet the standards
of skills, knowledge, values, and behavior that are expected of them for
membership in the mainstream, that is, middle-class America. It is not so
much a matter of talent as it is of how that talent presents itself through
conformity to a standard template of what is defined as a good student or,
at least, an adequate one. For example, performance on standardized tests,
with their emphasis on filling in the appropriate bubble rapidly with a
number 2 pencil, is far more important than creativity, initiative, and in-
dependent thinking. The most talented students who are unable to conform to this demand are not likely to succeed in school. Adequate performance on standardized tests, punctuality, participation when called upon,
proper deference to authority, and so on, are all requirements for avoid-
ing student failure. Students who learn how to "play the game" do not fail
in the sense of this social construct.

But some students, despite a deep reservoir of talent, cannot or will
not meet these standards. Disruptive social conditions in their homes and

communities, economic deprivation, difficult family relationships, and other experiences do not produce the types of middle-class behaviors that schools assume are necessary for academic success. Indeed, human survival in these situations may create adaptive behavior that is dysfunctional in a school situation. Acting tough and being ready to fight at the smallest slight are not acceptable in schools, and students who are goaded into action will experience school suspension or worse. But in some neighborhoods such readiness is a crucial tactic for survival. Conversely, studiousness and academic success may be perceived as signs of vulnerability, images that are to be avoided if one does not wish to be victimized by others.

In other cases, even if there is an ability to meet standards, there may be reluctance to do so. What is called socialization in the antiseptic world of academics is really a deliberate attempt to mold personalities in line with social expectations of what is thought of as competence (Dreeben, 1968; Inkeles, 1966). Some students refuse to be molded in the directions that are expected. Often, but not always, these students are drawn from minority, ethnic, or lower-income groups, and they view school as trying to change them in ways that they do not want to change and that alter their self-identities. They may also sense that even if they conform to what is expected, they will not succeed in what are unnatural roles for them. Some authors have referred to this as an oppositional culture in which students resist school conventions to maintain their own identities and sense of agency (Apple, 1979; Fordham, 1993; Giroux, 1981; Willis, 1977). Unfortunately, it often leads to school failure.

HOLDING STUDENTS TO STANDARDS

In the most fundamental sense, we have two choices as teachers. The first is to accept the standards set by our schools and society for all students and to try to help students meet those standards. Every teacher has a perception of what these standards are, a perception not only based on personal beliefs of what it takes to be successful in school and in adult life, but also imposed on us by our schools and society. We may not always agree with these standards, setting up a dilemma between our personal identities and what we perceive as our professional obligations.

Further, when it comes to school success or failure, it is not just our subjective view of how to measure these outcomes. Our schools and their governing institutions set out "official" measures to evaluate our students and, by implication, our efforts. For example, we may perceive that students should be familiar with poetry in its different forms and modes of expression and should be able to appreciate the meaning of poems and be able to write their own poetry when so inspired. But typical measures of student knowledge of poetry ask students to identify such forms as iambic pentameter and haiku or display a poem and ask students to identify the meaning intended by the author (rather than the reader) through multiple-choice responses. Paradoxically, students who love poetry and language and have a natural flair for poetic expression may do poorly on such measures, while those who lack such talents, but have refined their test-taking proficiencies, may do well.

Indeed, this is the danger of the present movement toward national standards. Any such standards must be universal, as witnessed by the term "national," and must be placed in a format that is easy to administer and inexpensive to score. This phenomenon raises the specter of schools that are less likely to focus on substantive knowledge and proficiency and demonstration of mastery than on teaching toward the instrumentality itself, the testing instrument and format. In my view, it is very unlikely that any approach based on national standards will get beyond the stultified instruments that are designed more for administrative convenience and economic feasibility than for evaluating the depth of understanding and use of knowledge.

In this respect, teachers face a challenge, even if they accept, in principle, existing standards or new ones that are imposed. At a conceptual level, they may agree with standards (e.g., all students should be proficient in understanding and using mathematics), but at the level of assessment the standard may mean something quite different (e.g., choosing the "correct" response in a multiple-choice test in a speedy manner). So, in adapting to standards for success, teachers are pushed to accept not only the conceptual domains and their contents, but also the way in which the standards are assessed by school authorities.

By narrowing both the theoretical standards for success and their current measures, teachers are restricted to a considerably narrower repertoire of teaching strategies than the universe available to them, and they are placed in a category that differs considerably from other professionals. The lawyer who defends or prosecutes an accused client may have a standard of success or failure (acquittal or conviction), but he or she has a very broad array of strategies to choose from in getting there, depending on his or her own strengths, the identity of the court, the jury, the characteristics of the accused, judicial precedent, and so on. Similarly, an abundant range of strategies is usually available to the artist, author, architect, mental health worker, physician, and other professionals faced with the challenge of meeting standards of success or failure in their endeavors. But for teachers there is likely to be the perpetual tension between the goals of teaching and learning and the narrow gauge of testing by which learning outcomes are assessed.

This tension is exacerbated by the fact that schools are under great pressure from their districts and other authorities to succeed on the basis of these narrow assessment criteria. Therefore, they look to adopt curriculum packages that are "teacher-resistant to change" if not actually "teacher-proofed." Such packages consist of not only textbooks that are to be rigorously adhered to, but student workbooks with drill-and-practice exercises, a teacher's guide that tells precisely what to do for each lesson with questions to raise and their answers, and quizzes that match up well in content and format to the standardized examinations used to measure student learning. In addition, staff development workshops are devoted to the proficient use of these packages. Again, we should ask what other profession is so constrained in its ability to benefit from experience, take risks, and make judgments in selecting strategies.

What if a teacher is willing to accept all of this in order to survive professionally? What can be done? This is often where the heroic teacher enters the scenario, best exemplified by a national figure like Jaime Escalantes, but existing in every locality (see the chapter by Barry Franklin). This is the teacher who visits a home to talk to the parents about helping the child or impresses upon the parent how much talent the child has; who foregoes lunches and arrives before school and stays after to work with students; who organizes extracurricular activities to provide students what they are lacking outside of the school; who purchases materials for the classroom and individual students; who advocates for them in the local community and among community agencies; who arranges special events such as field trips and guest speakers to inspire students and expose them to enriching experiences; who converts textbook-based curriculum into hands-on activities that connect with student experience and community life, and so on. Many teachers have undertaken at least some of these activities in the quest to help students succeed (for a personal experience, see the chapter by Susan Merrifield).

All of this requires taking tremendous risks, including the charge of being "out-of-compliance" with school regulations and decisions. Although such teachers want their students to do well on standardized tests and believe that such caring and enrichment will contribute to doing well, this may not be the case, for two reasons. First, students who are encouraged by such learning environments may see learning as being more than what is measured by standardized tests. They actually may develop a deep interest in subjects that is not consonant with preparing for the narrow testing formats and playing the game. Further, there will be a large number of students from at-risk situations who simply will be unable to take advantage of these opportunities to become more efficient learners. Although they may enjoy school more and appreciate the learning opportunities, circumstances such as having to work long hours to assist their families, involvement in gangs, peer pressure to resist the school regimen, unstable family situations, and insecure living conditions may overwhelm them.

A very poignant picture of the limits of heroic strategies is found in inner-city schools with high turnover. It is not unusual to find that in a given year, one-third to one-half of students who started school at the beginning of the year are no longer present by the end of the year, only to be replaced by other mobile students. In order to succeed educationally, students need a sustained experience in a supportive environment. But in these cases, the experience is short-lived and even confusing, as it may be in conflict with other, multiple experiences as students tumble from one school environment to another.

The point is that the best efforts of teachers to get students to meet the conventional standards may not succeed for many students, largely due to events beyond the control of the teachers. Yet, teachers are blamed both directly and obliquely for such failure, and they have the haunting suspicion that there might be something that they can do differently that will turn failure into success.

CHALLENGING THE STANDARDS

Getting students to meet standards that are highly contrived is a difficult challenge, both professionally and personally. Professionally, it may require heroic measures that do not work because of imposed curriculum packages and stultified systems of performance measurement that are in conflict with healthy conditions for learning; in addition, external conditions governing the lives of students over which teachers have little or no control may intervene. Personally, it subjects the teacher to potential conflict because the teacher's own judgments and perspectives on what should be learned and strategies for learning may be ignored or even contradicted by the enforced school regimen and compliance mentality. In this situation, teachers must consider confronting the standards themselves, not only standards of what constitutes success or failure, but standards of what constitutes acceptable practice (see the chapter by Eleanor Hilty).

It is virtually impossible for teachers to succeed in changing standards in their traditional roles as atomistic individuals. The reason is that teachers are part of a school culture and overall organizational system that imposes an overall standard for success or failure that is based on test scores and courses that are passed successfully. Although teachers can attempt to set different standards in the microcosm of their own classrooms, ones that are in greater harmony with their own educational beliefs and what they perceive as the needs of their students, ultimately the results will be judged by external standards that do not necessarily acknowledge or recognize their efforts. That is, if a larger arena is not changed, the standards are likely to remain the same. Teachers who attempt to single-handedly change the standards that define success or failure and teach toward those standards, are at risk personally and professionally in school systems that push toward compliance and conformity.

I believe that in the long run the reduction of failure for both teachers and students will necessitate a shift to more meaningful standards of both practice and outcomes, ones that we can agree should guide our work at levels that include, but go far beyond, the classroom. Although such a movement may begin at the level of the entire school, it ultimately must expand through networks of schools to alter the purview of society itself toward its schools and toward definitions and perceptions of success and failure. Several school restructuring movements are premised on changing the standards by which we judge success. The Coalition of Essential Schools under the leadership of Ted Sizer (1984) has set out nine principles that it asks schools to discuss in a democratic discourse and to apply in their communities. These standards include values like decency and the demonstration of student proficiency through performance on meaningful or authentic tasks rather than artificial and contrived testing instruments. Expeditionary Learning Outward Bound is a second example. It views learning as an "expedition" in which teachers and students working together use in-depth, investigative fieldwork to learn, while stressing the values of service and the power of challenging physical experience in the outdoors.[1]

Our own movement, Accelerated Schools (Hopfenberg, Levin, & Associates, 1993; Levin, 1996), also views standards and how they should be accomplished as open to democratic discourse at the school site. Of course, such a discourse should be an informed one that provides the participants with access to information on what is known about fruitful approaches to child development, citizenship, productive work, and family life, as well as the growth of a healthy intellect. Indeed, one can conceive of the movement toward national standards as an informational one that provides valuable insights and a knowledge base that informs local discourse on what is desirable from the different perspectives.

PRINCIPLES AND VALUES FOR CREATING STANDARDS

The goal of the Accelerated School is to bring all students into a meaningful educational mainstream, where school staff and parents can create, for all students, the dream school they would want for their own children, reflecting strong overtones of John Dewey. At the middle school level, students must be included in this endeavor. The emphasis is on creating an intrinsically meaningful educational experience and results based on decisions of those involved in the educational process, including students, teachers, parents, and other school staff and community members. This goal places a great deal of responsibility on educational communities to both design and create optimal school environments. In order to accomplish this, an Accelerated School enlists three central principles to guide all of its activities: (1) unity of purpose; (2) empowerment with responsibility; and (3) building on strengths.

Unity of Purpose

Unity of purpose refers to the common purpose and practices of the school in behalf of all its children. Traditional schools separate children according to abilities, learning challenges, and other distinctions; staff are divided according to their narrow teaching, support, or administrative functions; and parents usually are relegated only the most marginal of roles in the education of their children. Accelerated Schools require that the schools forge a unity of purpose around the education of all students and all members of the school community, a living vision and culture of working together in behalf of all of the children. Strict separation of either teaching or learning roles works against this unity and results in different expectations for different groups of children. Accelerated Schools formulate and work toward high expectations for all children, and children adopt these high standards for themselves.

Empowerment with Responsibility

Empowerment with responsibility refers to who makes the educational decisions and takes responsibility for their consequences. Traditional schools rely on the rules, regulations, guidelines, directives, policies, and mandates of higher authorities at school district and state levels, as well as on compliance with the contents of textbooks and instructional packages adopted by states and local districts, but formulated by publishers who are far removed from schools. Staff at the school site have little discretionary power over most of the major curriculum and instructional practices of the school, and students and parents have almost no meaningful input into school decisions. This sense of powerlessness leads to a feeling of exclusion in terms of the ability to influence the major dimensions of school life. Worst of all, almost all of the mandated practices have been shown to be demonstrably ineffective in terms of beneficial academic results and healthy child development.

An Accelerated School requires that school staff, parents, and students take responsibility for the major decisions that will determine educational outcomes. The school is no longer a place in which roles, responsibilities, practices, and curriculum content are determined by forces beyond the control of its members. In its daily operations, the school community hones its unity of purpose through making and implementing the decisions that will determine its destiny. At the same time, the school takes responsibility for the consequences of its decisions through continuous assessment and accountability, holding as its ultimate purpose its vision of what the school will become. This is accomplished through a parsimonious, but highly effective, system of governance and problem solving that ensures inclusion of students, staff, and parents in the daily life of the school. The school is provided with the capacity to make and implement informed decisions and to assess their consequences.

Building on Strengths

Traditionally, schools have been far more assiduous about identifying the weaknesses of their students than looking for their strengths. A focus on weaknesses or deficiencies leads naturally to organizational and instructional practices in which children are tracked according to common deficiencies. The logic is that "lower" groups cannot keep up with a curricular pace that is appropriate for higher groups. But Accelerated Schools begin by identifying strengths of participants and building on those strengths to overcome areas of weakness.

In this respect, all students are treated as gifted and talented, because the gifts and talents of each child are sought out and recognized. Such strengths are used as a basis for providing enrichment and acceleration. As soon as one recognizes that all students have strengths and weaknesses, a simply stratification of students no longer makes sense. Strengths include not only the various areas of intelligence identified by Howard Gardner (1983), but also areas of interest, curiosity, motivation, and knowledge that grow out of the culture, experiences, and personalities of all children. Classroom themes can be those in which children show interest and curiosity and in which reciprocal teaching, cooperative learning, peer and cross-age tutoring, and individual and group projects can highlight the unique talents of each child in classroom and school activities. These group processes and the use of specialized staff can both recognize and build on the particular strengths and contributions of each child, while providing assistance in areas of need within the context of meaningful academic work.

Accelerated Schools require that each child be fully included in the activities of the school, while validating individual strengths and addressing areas of special need (see the chapter by Susan Peters, Alan Klein, and Catherine Shadwick). This can be done in regular classrooms employing classroom-wide and school-wide curricular approaches that are based on inclusion of all children in the central life of the school. It can be done not only with multiability grouping, but by recognizing that all children have different profiles of strengths that can be used to complement each other and to create strong teams that provide internal reinforcement among students.

It also should be noted that the process of building on strengths is not limited to students. Accelerated Schools build on the strengths of parents, teachers, and other school staff. Parents can be powerful allies if they are placed in productive roles and provided with the skills to work with their own children. Teachers bring gifts of insight, intuition, and organizational acumen to the instructional process, gifts that often are untapped by the mechanical curricula that are so typical of remedial programs. By acknowledging the strengths found among participants within the entire school community, all participants are expected to contribute to success.

Accelerated School Values

Accelerated Schools acknowledge a set of values that increasingly must be incorporated into relationships and activities as the school develops. These include the school as a center of expertise, equity, community, risk taking, experimentation, reflection, participation, trust, and communication. Virtually all of these focus on the inner power, vision, capabilities, and solidarity of the school community rather than dependency on external forces. Especially important are such values as equity, the view that the school has an obligation to all children to create for them the dream school that we would want for our own children. Such a school must treat children equitably and must address equitable participation and outcomes. The school is viewed as an overall community rather than as a building with many separate communities represented, although the cultures and experiences of different students are acknowledged and incorporated into the school experience. Addressing the needs of all children will require experimentation and risk taking, reflection, trust, and communication. Above all, the concept of unity of purpose is present in all of the values and practices of the school, a necessary approach to inclusion of all students in a common school dream.

Powerful Learning

The three principles and nine values of Accelerated Schools are used to create powerful learning situations. A powerful learning situation is one that incorporates changes in school organization, climate, curriculum, and instructional strategies to build on the strengths of students, staff, and community in order to create an optimal learning situation. It is based on a constructivist theory of learning that assumes that students construct their own understanding from their experiences. Accordingly, the richness and completeness of experiences provided to children are key to their ability to learn and make sense of the world. This approach lies at the base of most of the recent progress in science and mathematics education, as well as other subjects. What is unique about the powerful learning approach is that changes are not piecemeal, but integrated around all aspects of the learning situation. This conflicts sharply with the usual attempts to transform schools through idiosyncratic reforms involving the ad hoc adoption of different curriculum packages, instructional practices, and organizational changes to address separately each perceived problem that the school faces.

In contrast, powerful learning is based on a perspective in which the conditions must be created for children to construct their own understanding of ideas in all of the academic domains, as well as social institutions, human relationships, and emotions. It is based on making connections between the interests, culture, and experiences of children and their many abilities in an environment that requires active participation on their part (Hopfenberg, Levin, & Associates, 1993, Chs. 6–9). Typical activities include investigation, exploration, hypothesis generation and testing, artistic expression, discussion, debate, search and interpretation of knowledge bases, and projects that integrate many of these activities as well as the traditional school subjects into a focused result. Powerful learning builds on the strengths of all community members and empowers them to be proactive learners by developing skills through intrinsically challenging activities that require both groupwork and individual endeavor.

Accelerated Schools also emphasize the connections between the big wheels of the school and the little ones. The big wheels refer to the overall school philosophy and change process that are shared collaboratively by all members of the school community and that are transformed into school-wide activities. The small wheels refer to the informal innovations that grow out of participation by individuals or small groups in embracing the school's philosophy and change process. These little wheels result from the internalization of the school philosophy and change process into the belief system of school members, bringing about changes in their individual decisions and commitments in classrooms and in individual and group interactions.

The three principles, the values, and the powerful learning approach of Accelerated Schools enable schools to set their own standards, with participation of students and parents. In addition, they provide a system of governance and decision making through inquiry that enables schools to reach those standards. By building on strengths, they allow the possibility of success for both students and teachers rather than setting out narrow criteria for success that must necessarily be based on a particular type of student strength and a narrow range of standards measured in conventional ways.

It is not the purpose of this chapter to present the process by which schools transform themselves into Accelerated Schools, since details are readily available (e.g., Hopfenberg, Levin, & Associates, 1993; Levin, 1996). The bottom line is that schools as democratic communities can create their own informed standards that they also can reach through democratic governance and practices. In this way, all teachers and students can succeed in creating entire schools in which the big wheels of school policy and governance are aligned and support the smaller wheels of individual classrooms toward a common set of goals that may be reached in different ways for different students and different teachers. Such schools can be the building blocks of a larger movement that respects and nurtures both student and teacher talent so that failure is a rare event and talent development for all is the dominant theme (Brian DeLany's chapter takes a more pessimistic stance).

CREATIVE TENSION

Until that time that school communities can agree on standards and have the organizational acumen to enable virtually all students to reach those standards, we return to more conventional settings where teachers are faced with preparing students for standards that are determined in a manner largely external to the school. In that setting there will always be personal and professional tensions faced by both students and teachers, for reasons set out earlier. While those tensions have a downside, they also can be a source of pressure for change. For within these tensions lies the persistent question asked by many teachers: Could I have done something different that would have prevented failure? What if I changed the lesson? What if I had given him more time for assignments, given his limited English? What if I had called a social service agency, given the rumors that I heard about her living conditions? What if I had taken more interest in his situation or had taken more time with him? Could she have succeeded if I had drawn on her culture?

Such self-doubt on the teachers' part can serve as a creative tension—albeit a very distressing one—if we are to move in a different direction. Ultimately, teachers must begin to recognize that individual responses to relieve the tensions will always have limited results, for it is a system failure that looms much larger than an individual failure. Of course, some teachers are ill-suited to teach or lack the knowledge, insights, and commitment to succeed; some individual students willfully fail for reasons that are beyond the capacity of schools, families, and communities to intervene in. But the use of inappropriately limited standards and measures of success to screen and sort students must be viewed as a larger challenge than just that of individual teachers and students failing. The widespread use of teacher-resistant curriculum packages that fail to connect with student experience and culture and that fail to capitalize on teacher and student strengths is a system failure. The lack of resources and time for working collaboratively with other school staff and parents does not derive from decisions of individual students and parents. This does not suggest in any way that individual students and individual teachers have no responsibilities until there are changes in the system. We all have some capacity for making decisions in our lives and taking responsibility for our activities to achieve success as structured by the present schooling system or some deviation from that system that we believe is merited. But until we shift a major part of the focus on failure to the need to transform entire schools, school districts, and state and national educational systems to democratic entities that are designed for the success of all participants, we ourselves will fail to alleviate much of the cause of present student and teacher failure.

NOTE

1. This is one of the seven projects sponsored by the New American School Development Corporation (NASDC). Information can be obained from Expeditionary Learning Outward Bound, 122 Mount Auburn St., Cambridge, MA 02138.

REFERENCES

Apple, M. (1979). *Ideology and curriculum*. London: Routledge & Kegan Paul.
Dreeben, R. (1968). *On what is learned in school*. Reading, MA: Addison-Wesley.
Fordham, S. (1993). Racelessness as a factor in Black students' school success: pragmatic strategy or pyrrhic victory? In H. S. Shapiro & D. Purpel (Eds.), *Critical social issues in American education* (pp. 129–178). New York: Longman.
Gardner, H. (1983). *Frames of mind: The theory of multiple intelligences*. New York: Basic Books.
Giroux, H. A. (1981). *Ideology, culture, and the process of schooling*. Philadelphia: Temple University Press.
Hopfenberg, W., Levin, H. M., & Associates. (1993). *The Accelerated Schools resource guide*. San Francisco: Jossey-Bass.

Inkeles, A. (1966). Social structure and the socialization of competence. *Harvard Educational Review, 36,* 265–283.

Levin, H. M. (1996). Accelerated schools after eight years. In L. Schauble & R. Glaser (Eds.), *Innovations in learning: New environments for education* (pp. 329–352). Mahwah, NJ: Erlbaum.

Lortie, D. (1975). *Schoolteacher: A sociological study.* Chicago: University of Chicago Press.

Sizer, T. R. (1984). *Horace's compromise: The dilemma of the American high school.* Boston: Houghton Mifflin.

Willis, P. (1977). *Learning to labor.* Lexington, MA: Heath.

About the Editor and the Contributors

Richard J. Altenbaugh is a faculty member in the College of Education at Slippery Rock University.

Brian DeLany is an Associate Professor of Educational Policy Analysis in the Department of Teacher Education at Michigan State University.

Barry M. Franklin (Editor) is a Professor and Chair of the Department of Education, a member of the Faculty Council of the Program in African American Studies, and a faculty member of the Program in Public Administration at the University of Michigan–Flint.

Eleanor Blair Hilty is an Assistant Professor of Educational Foundations in the Department of Administration, Curriculum, and Instruction in the School of Education at Western Carolina University.

Alan Klein is a doctoral candidate in school psychology at Michigan State University.

Henry M. Levin is the David Jacks Professor of Higher Education and Economics at Stanford University and a Visiting Scholar at the Russell Sage Foundation.

Susan R. Merrifield is an Associate Professor of English Education at Lesley College.

Susan J. Peters is an Associate Professor of Education in the Department of Counseling, Educational Psychology, and Special Education and the Department of Teacher Education at Michigan State University.

Catherine Shadwick is a special education teacher in the Flint, Michigan Community Schools.

Lynda Stone is an Associate Professor of Education at the University of North Carolina–Chapel Hill.

Index